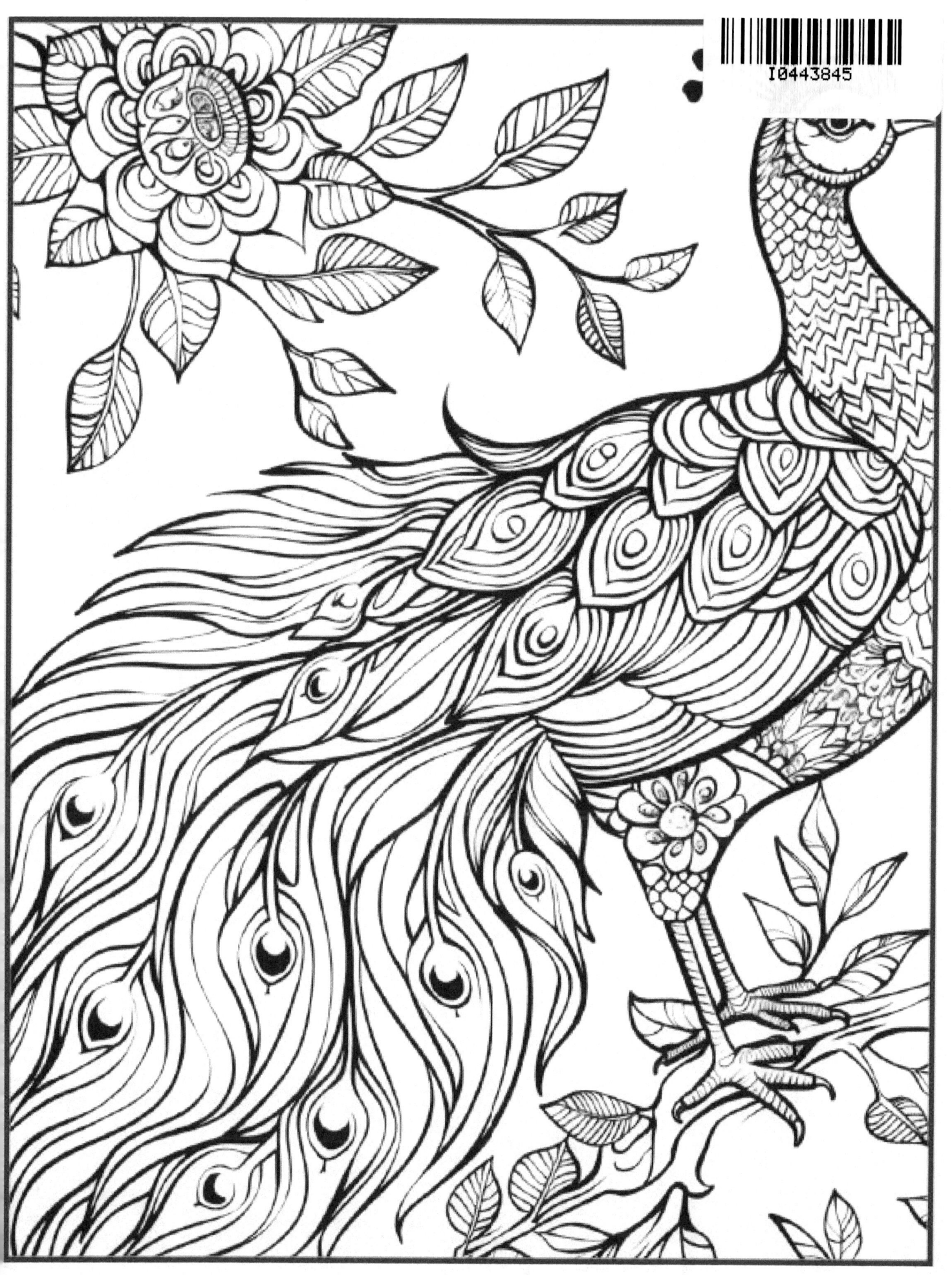

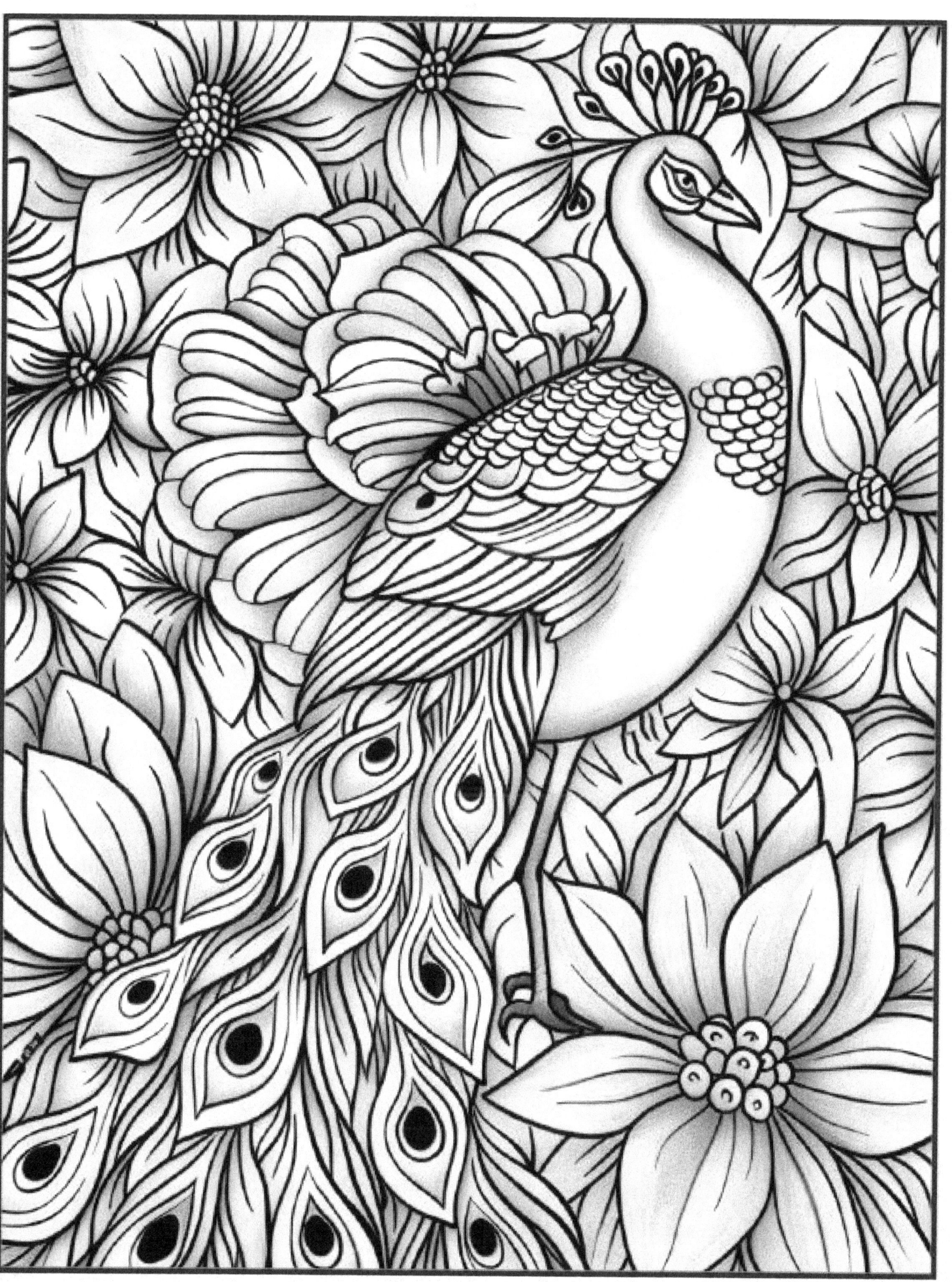

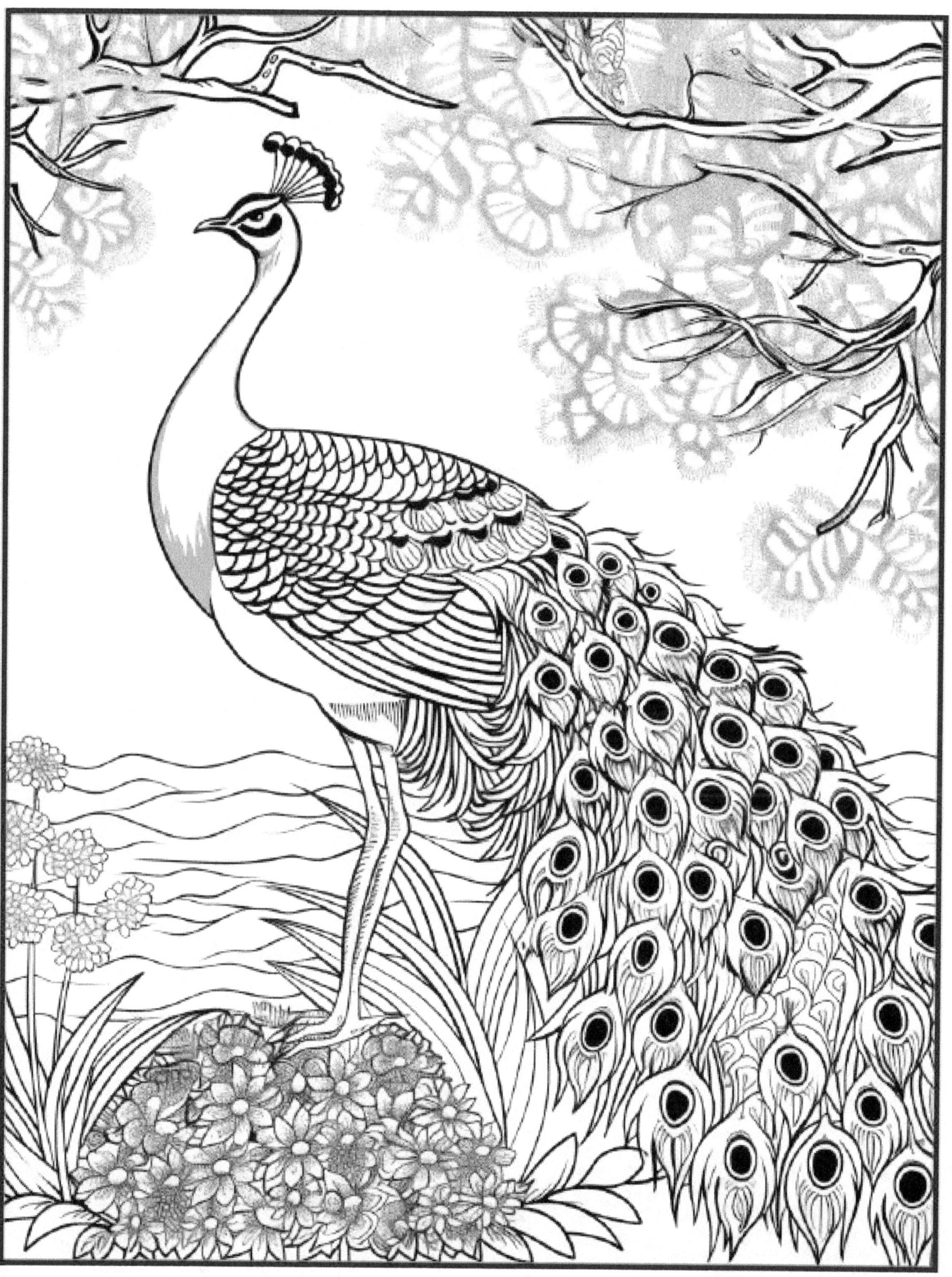

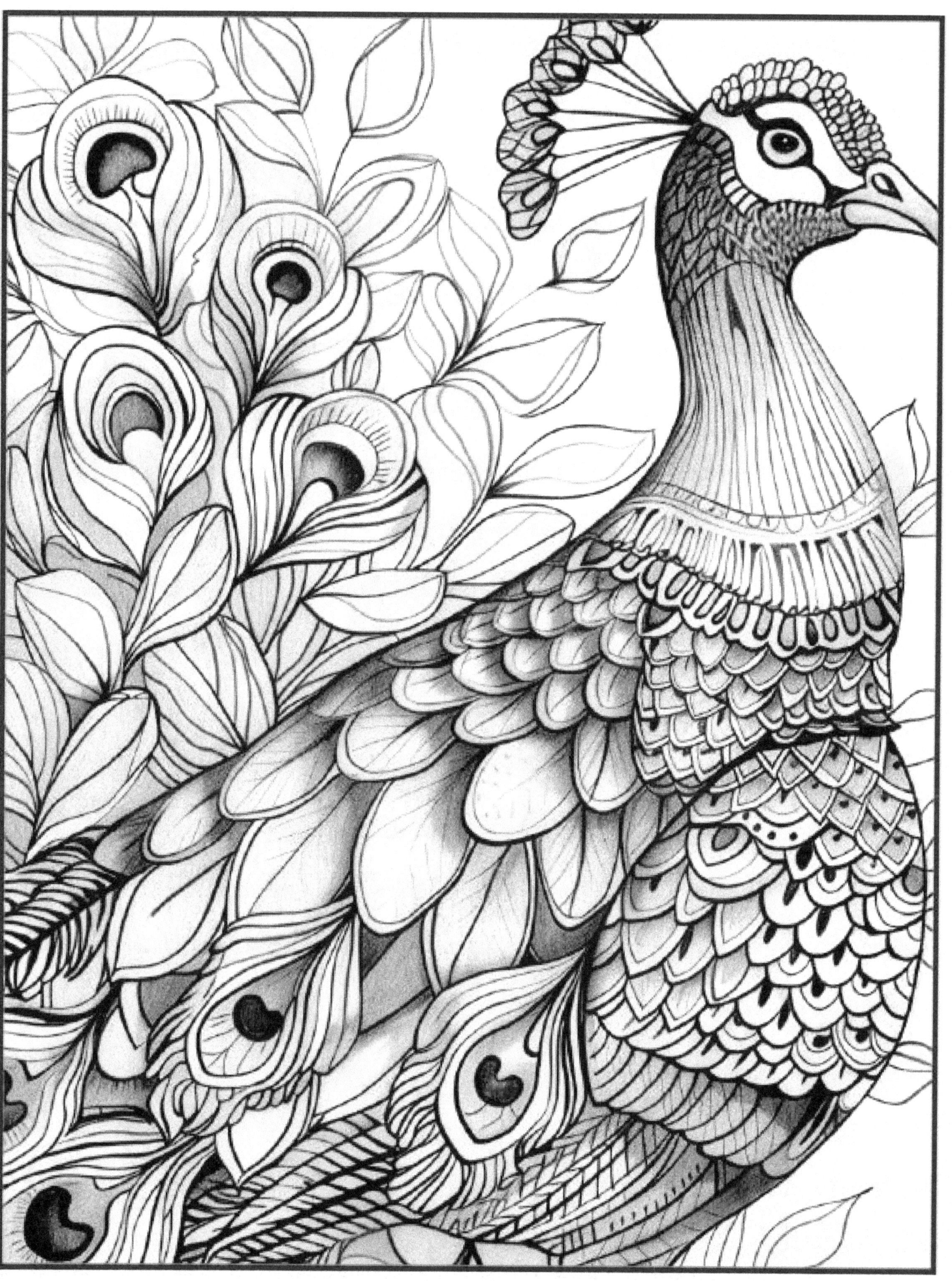

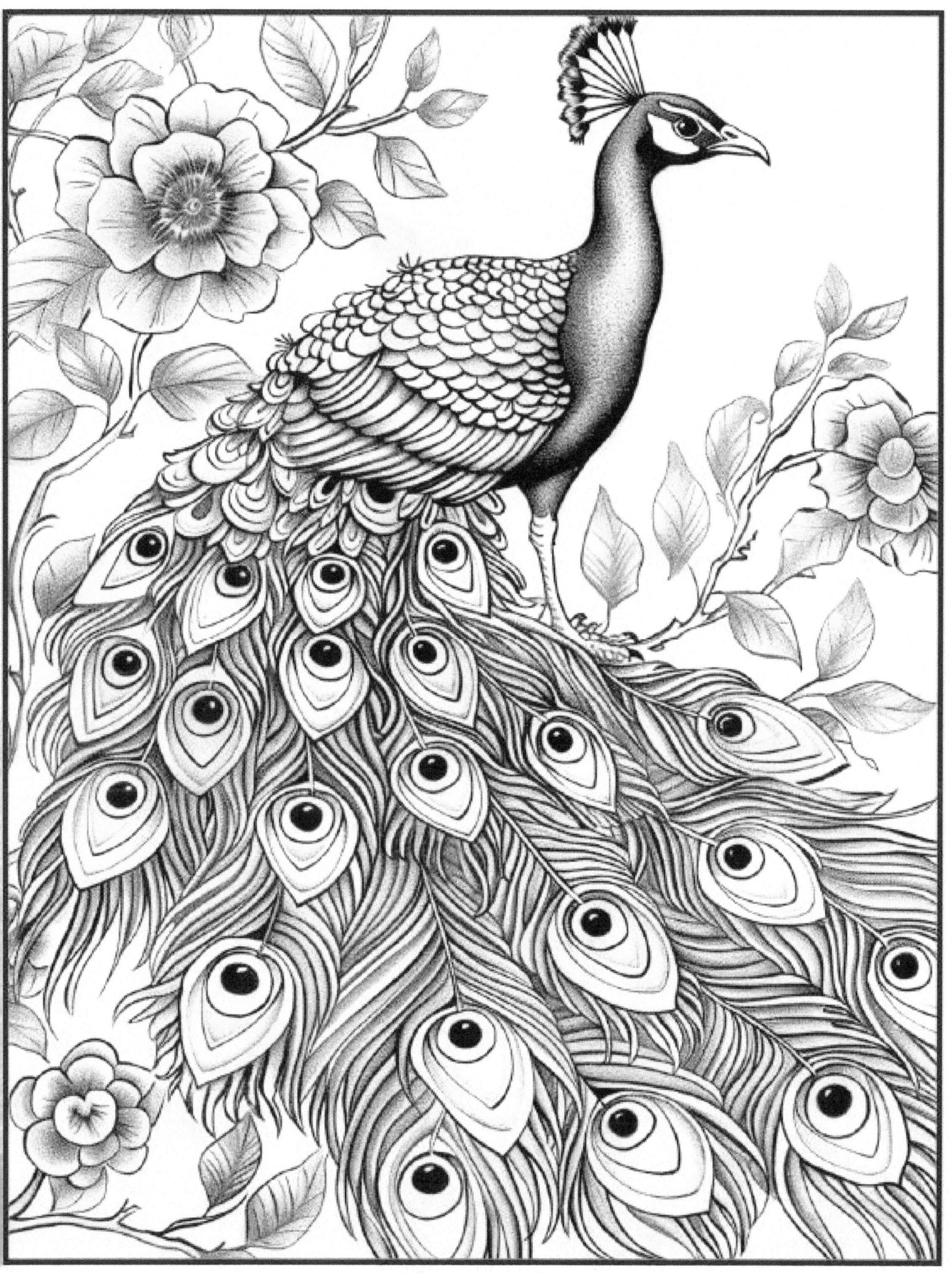

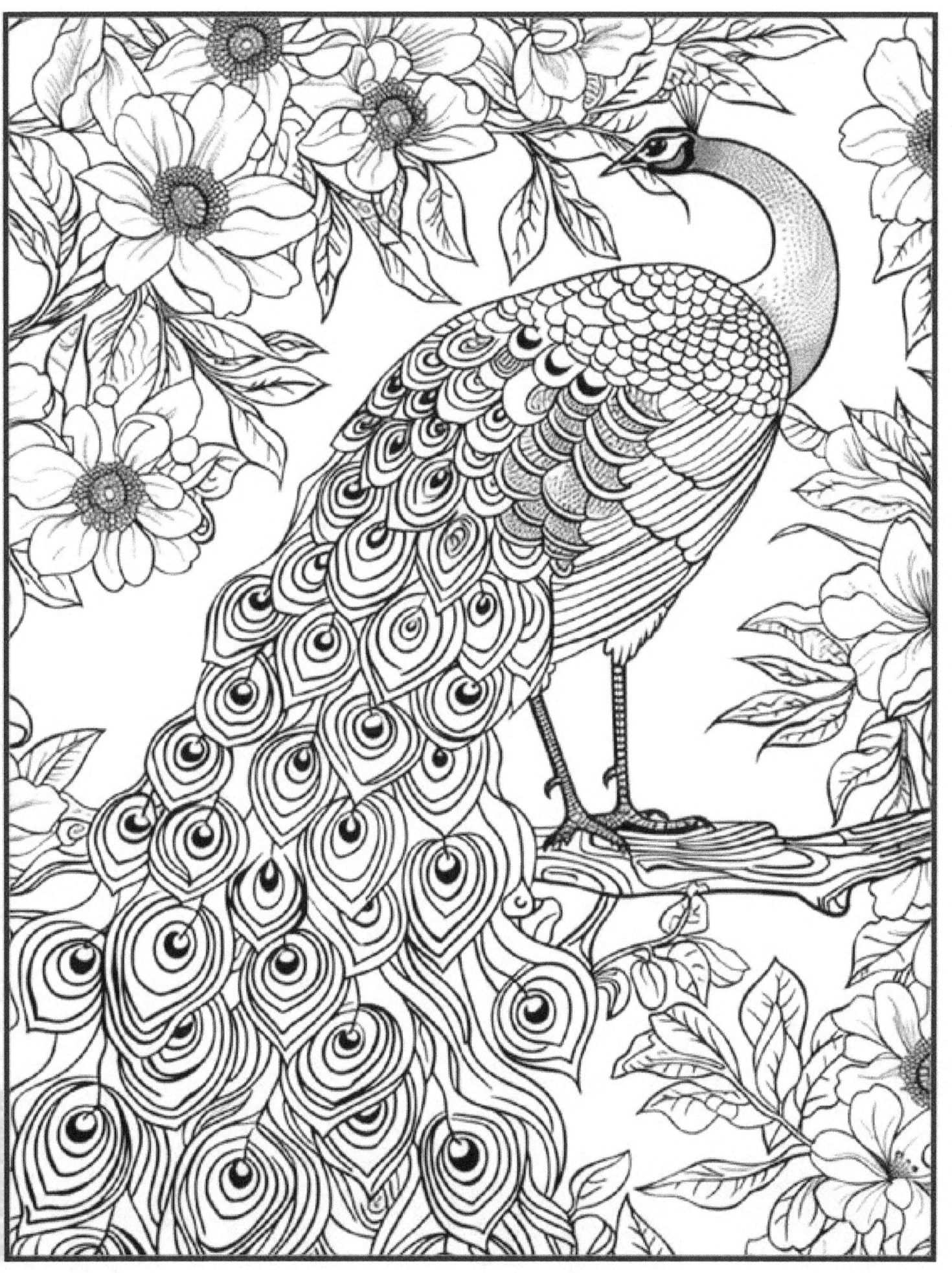

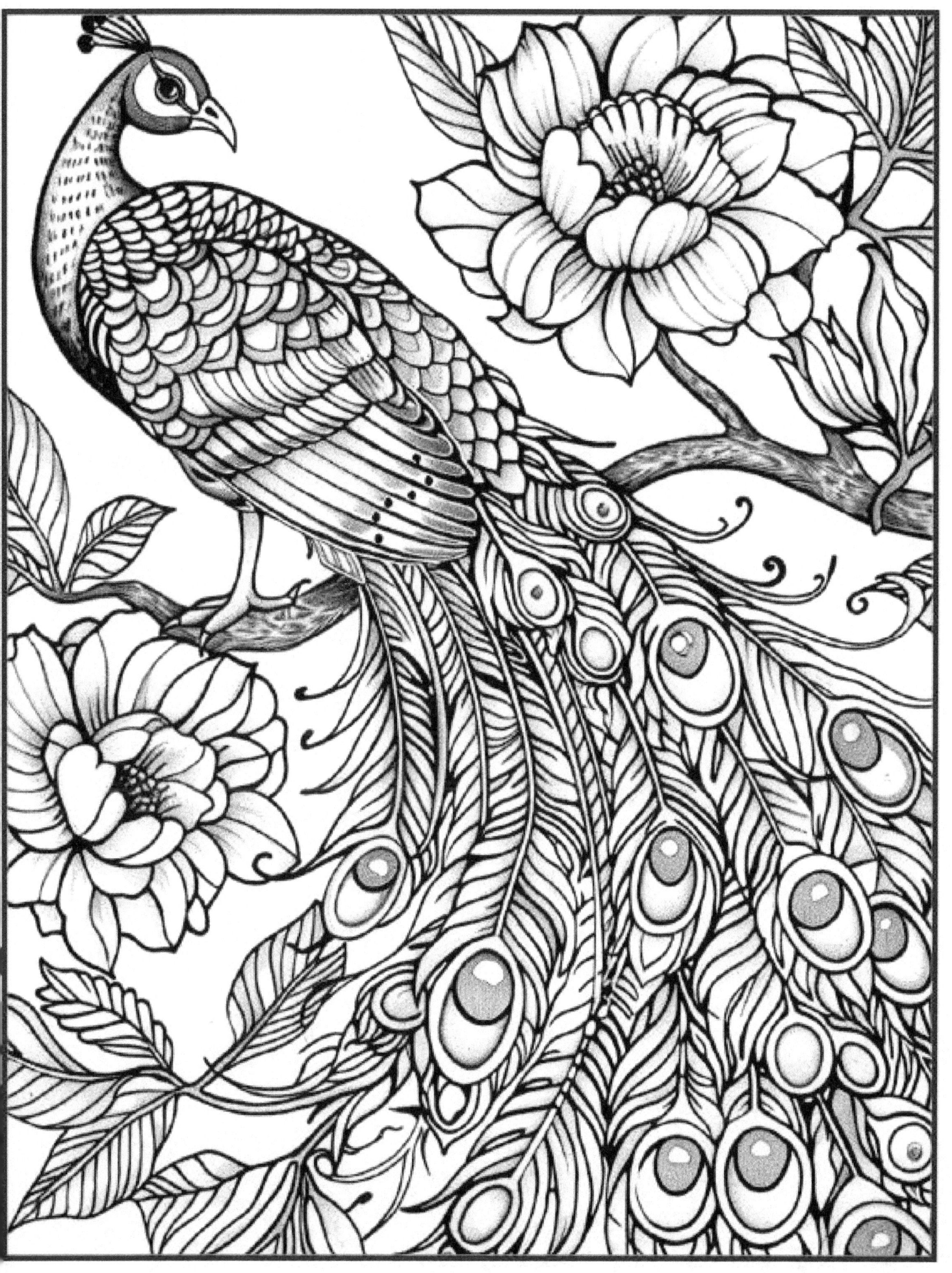

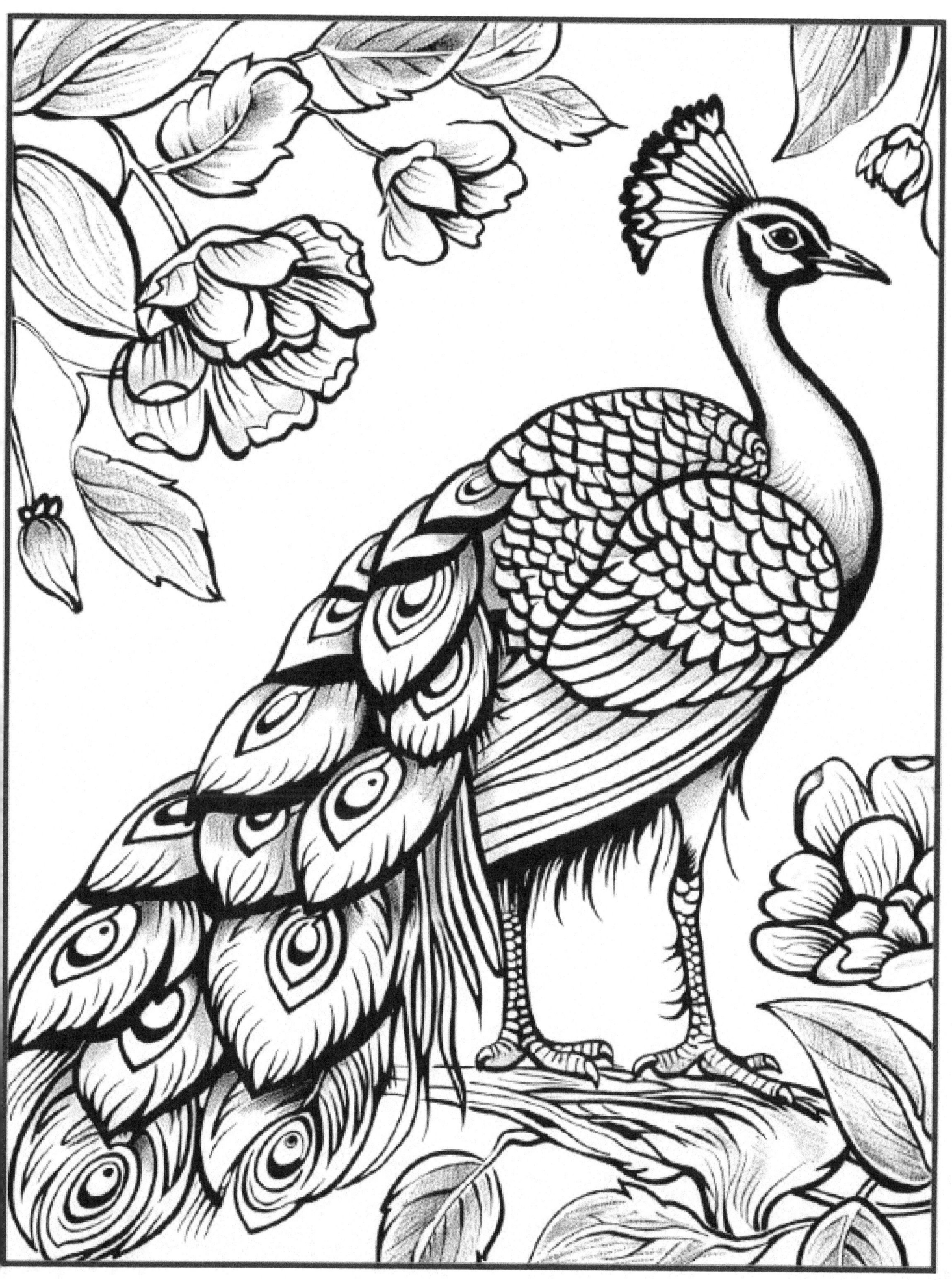

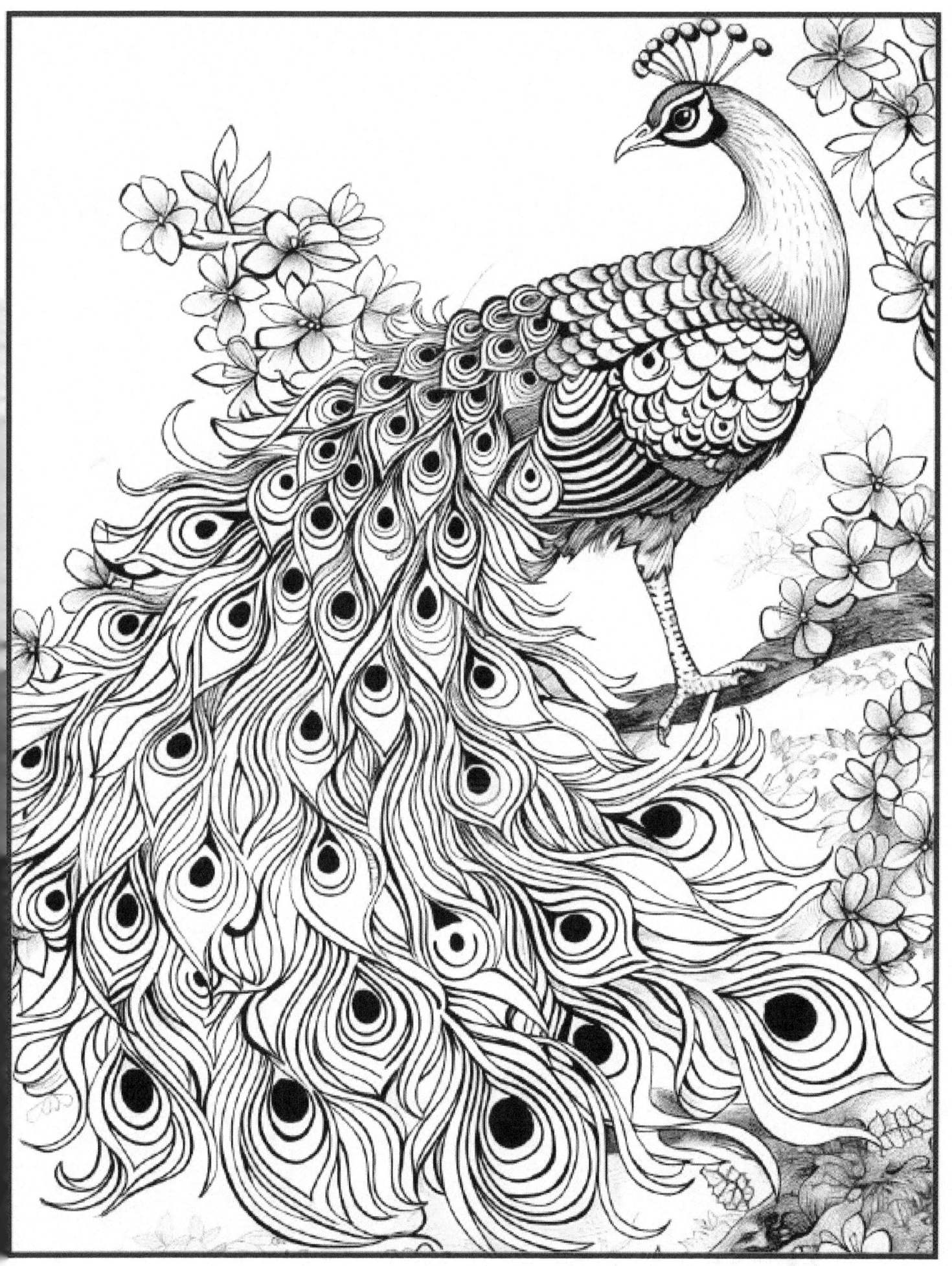

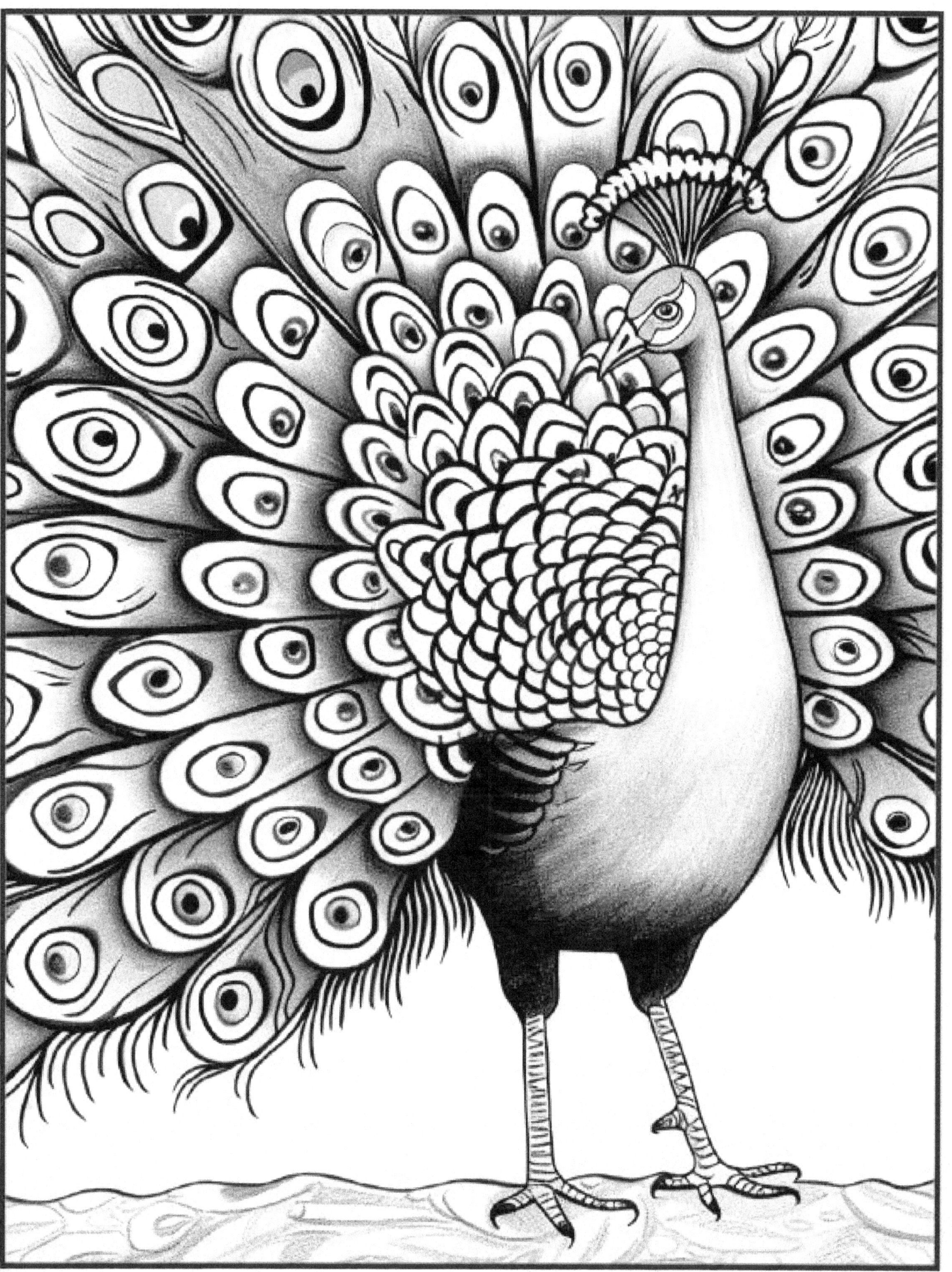

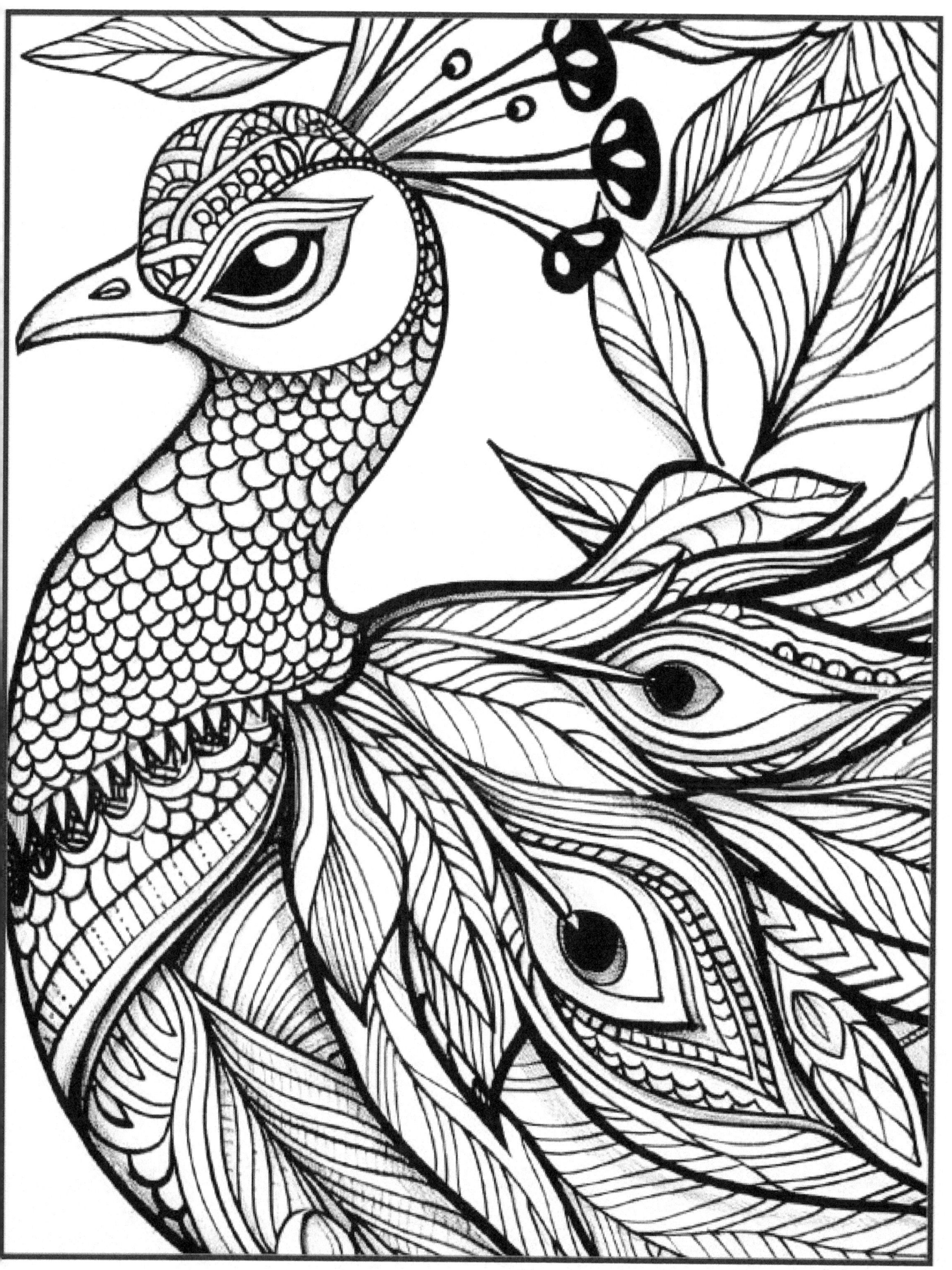

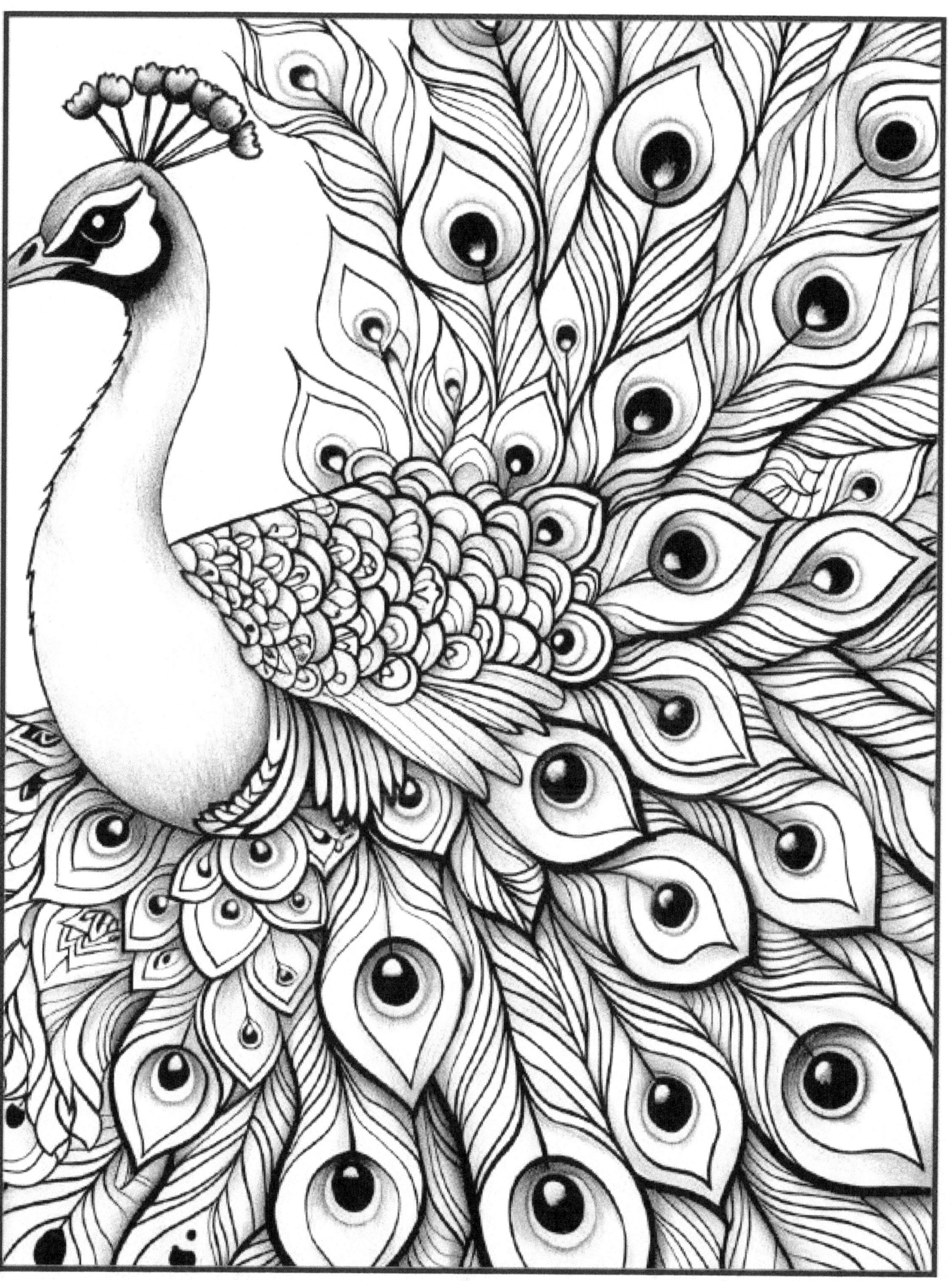

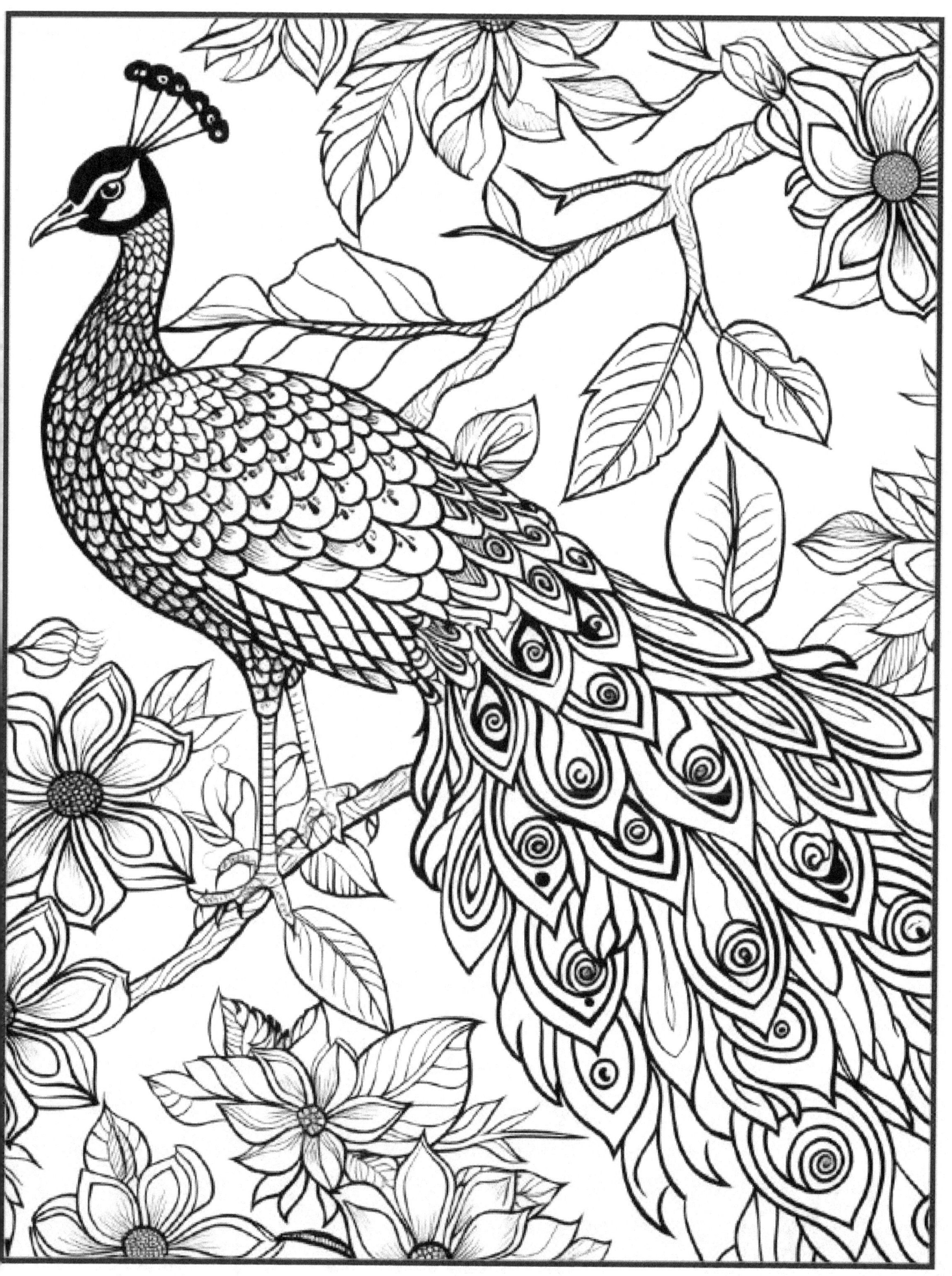

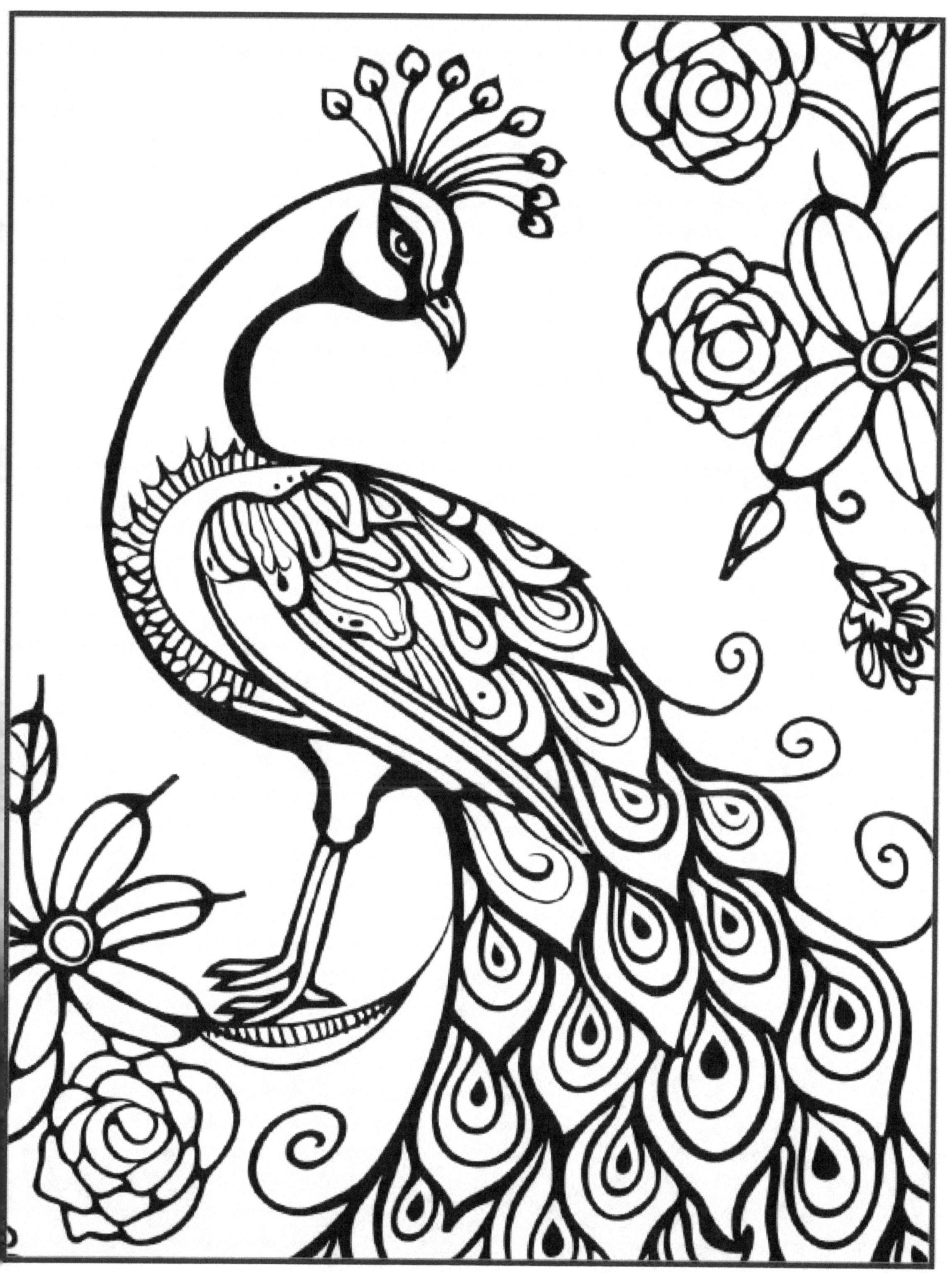

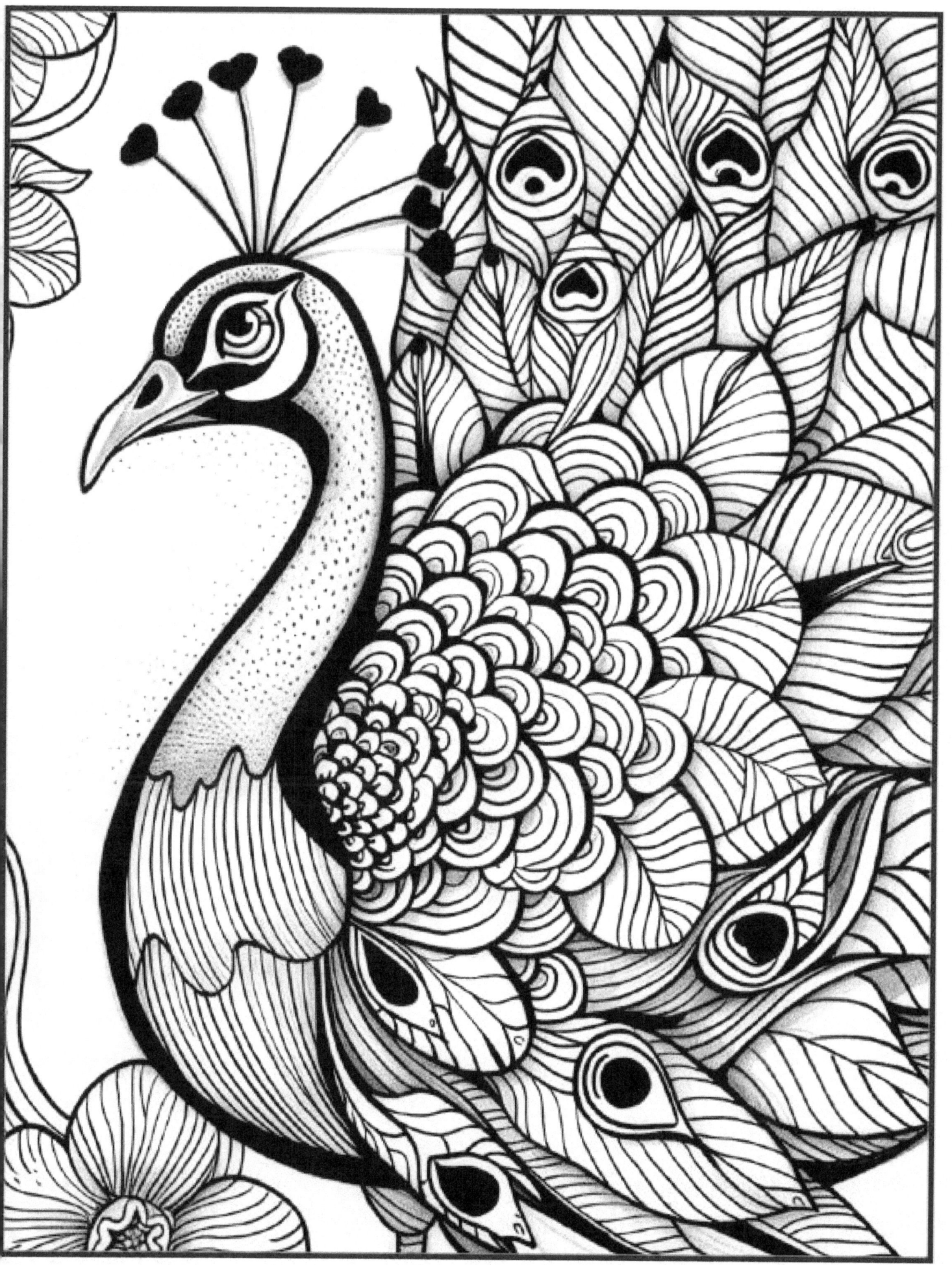

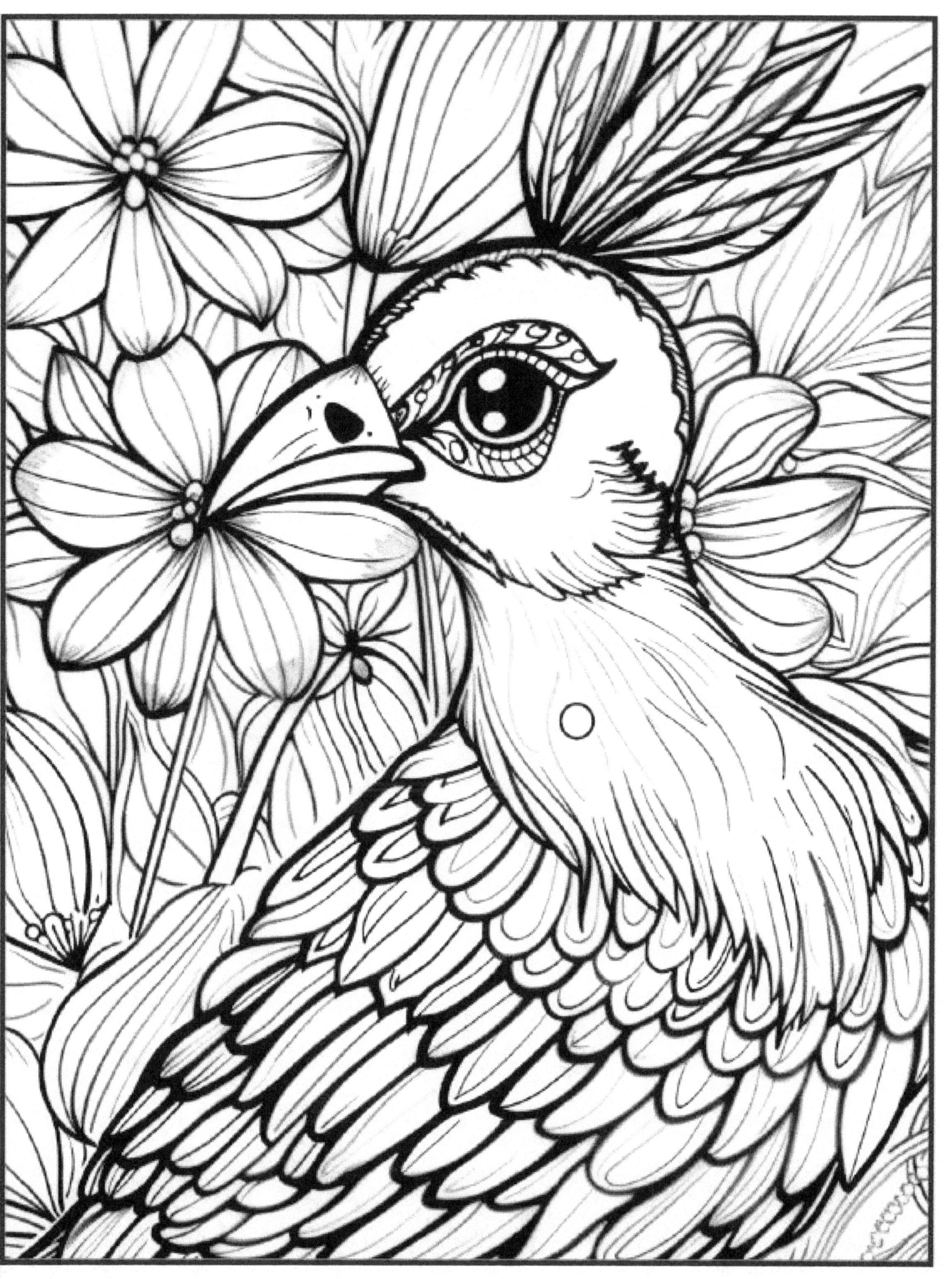

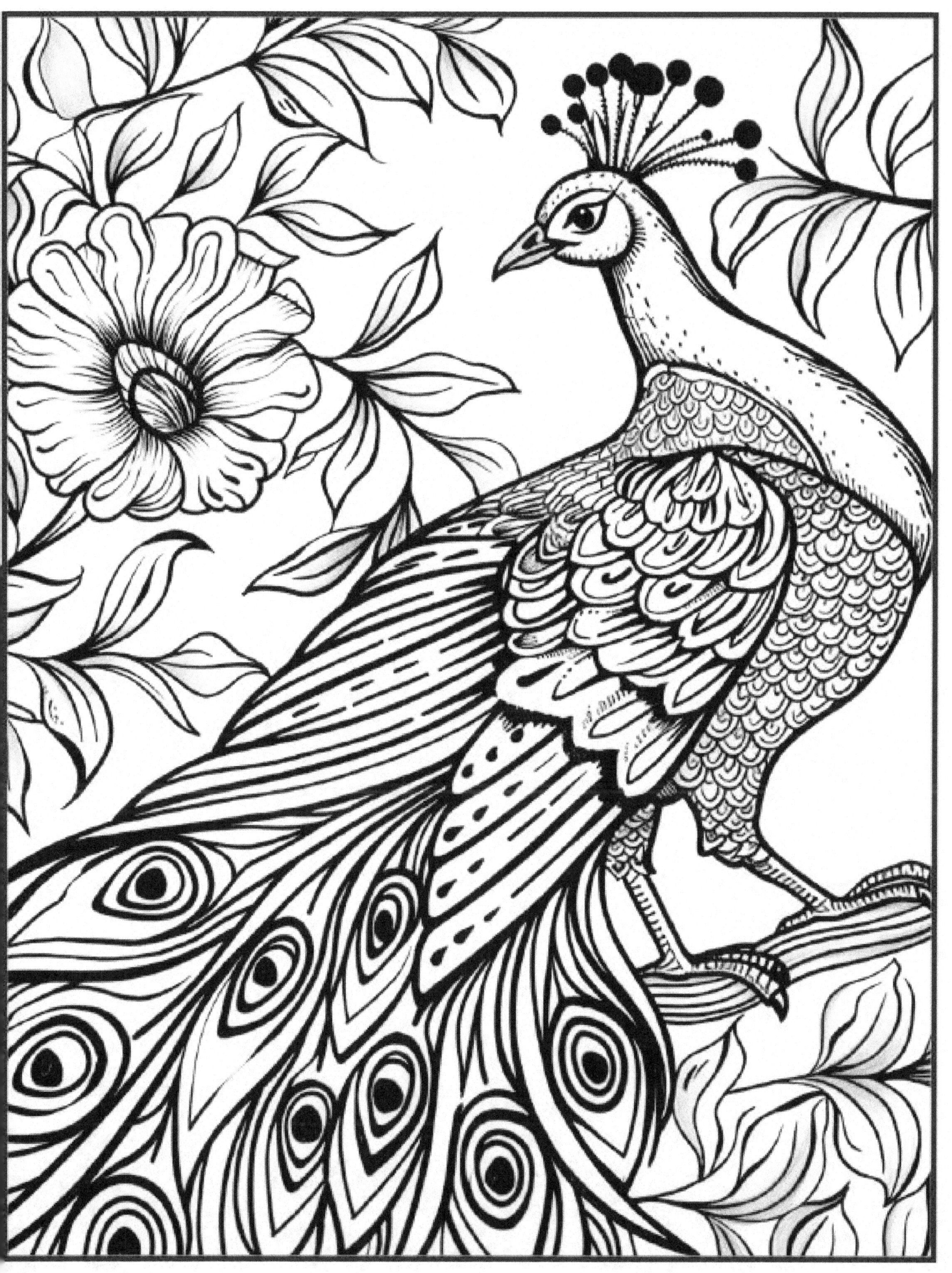

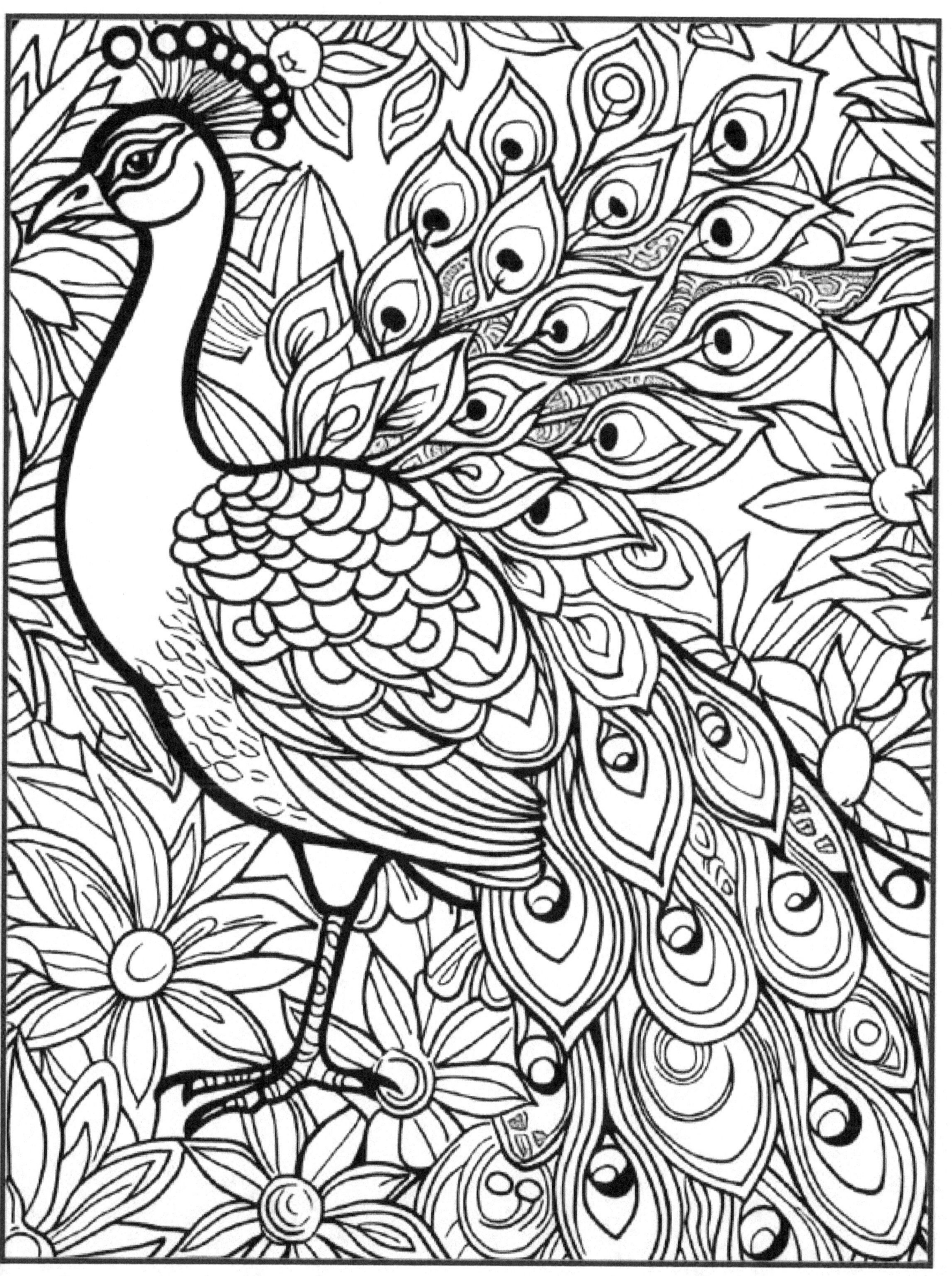

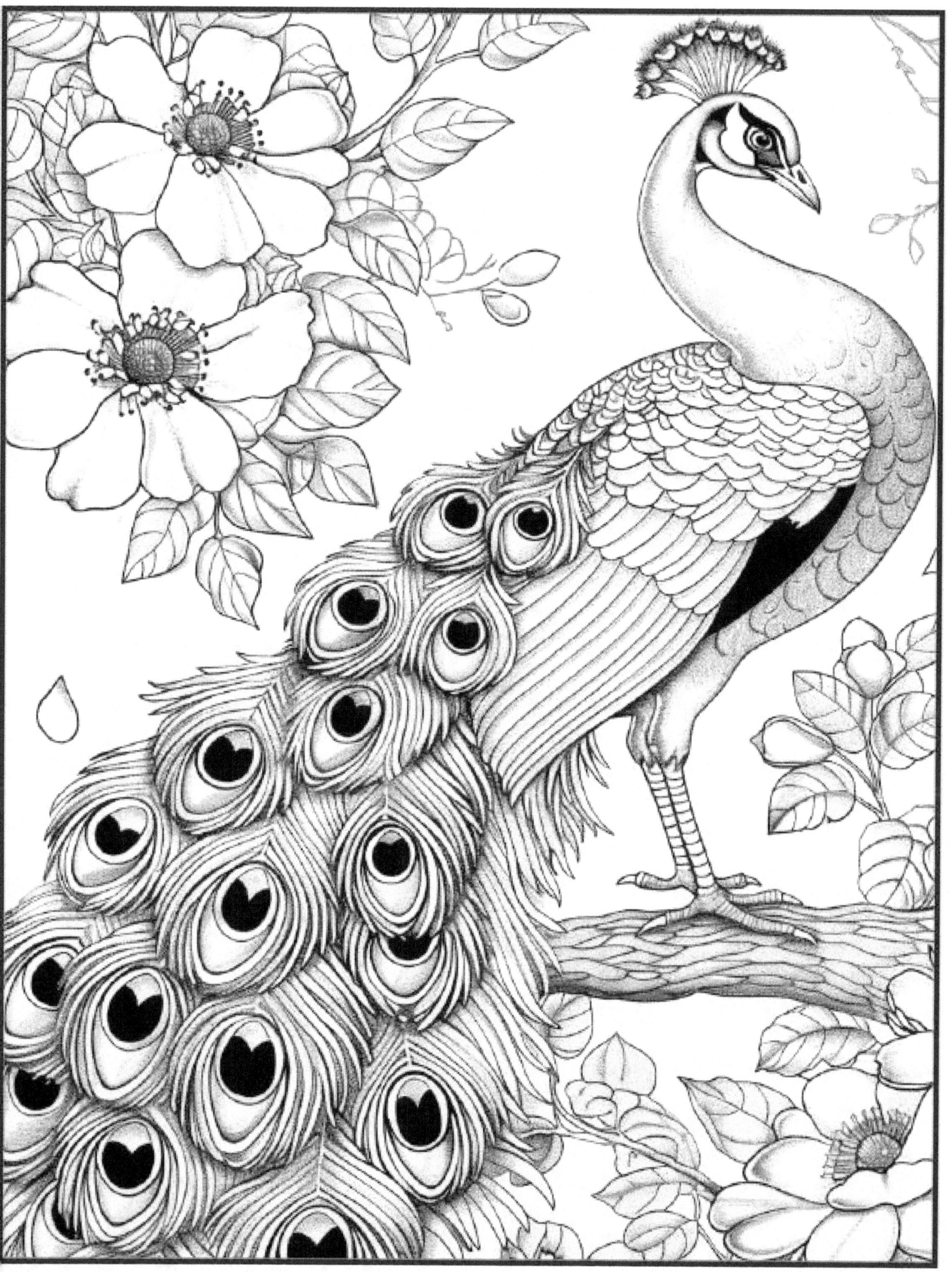

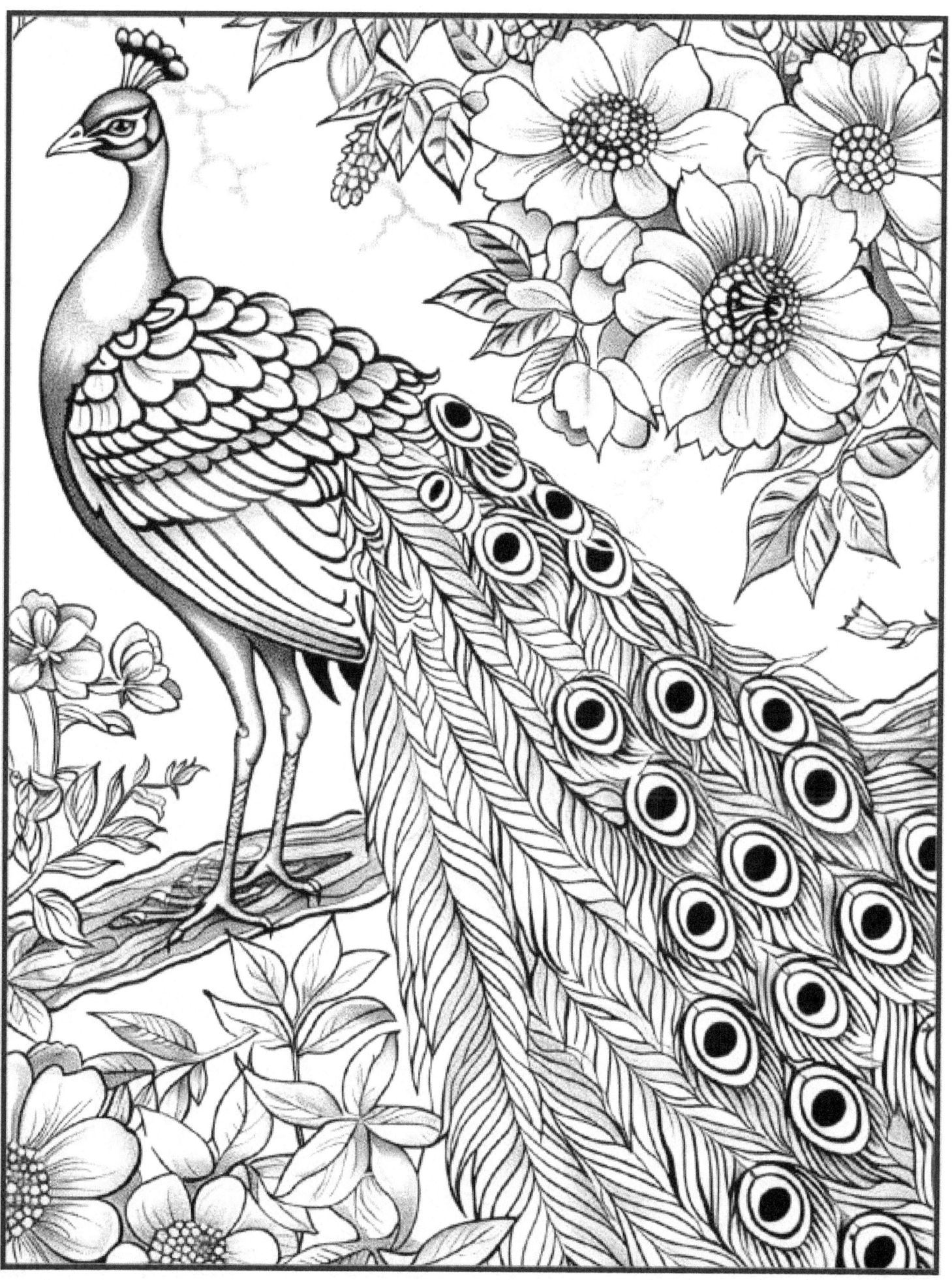

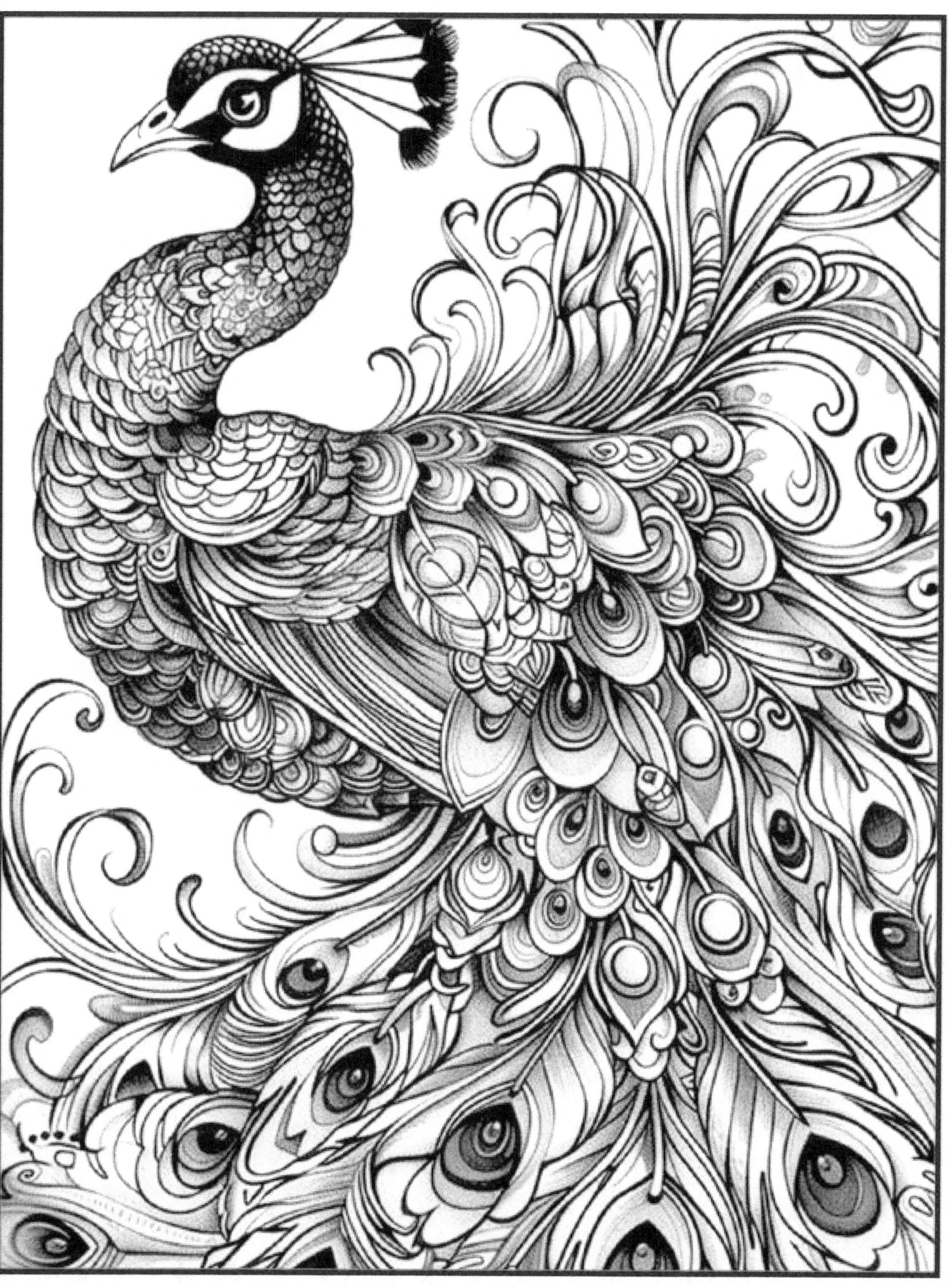

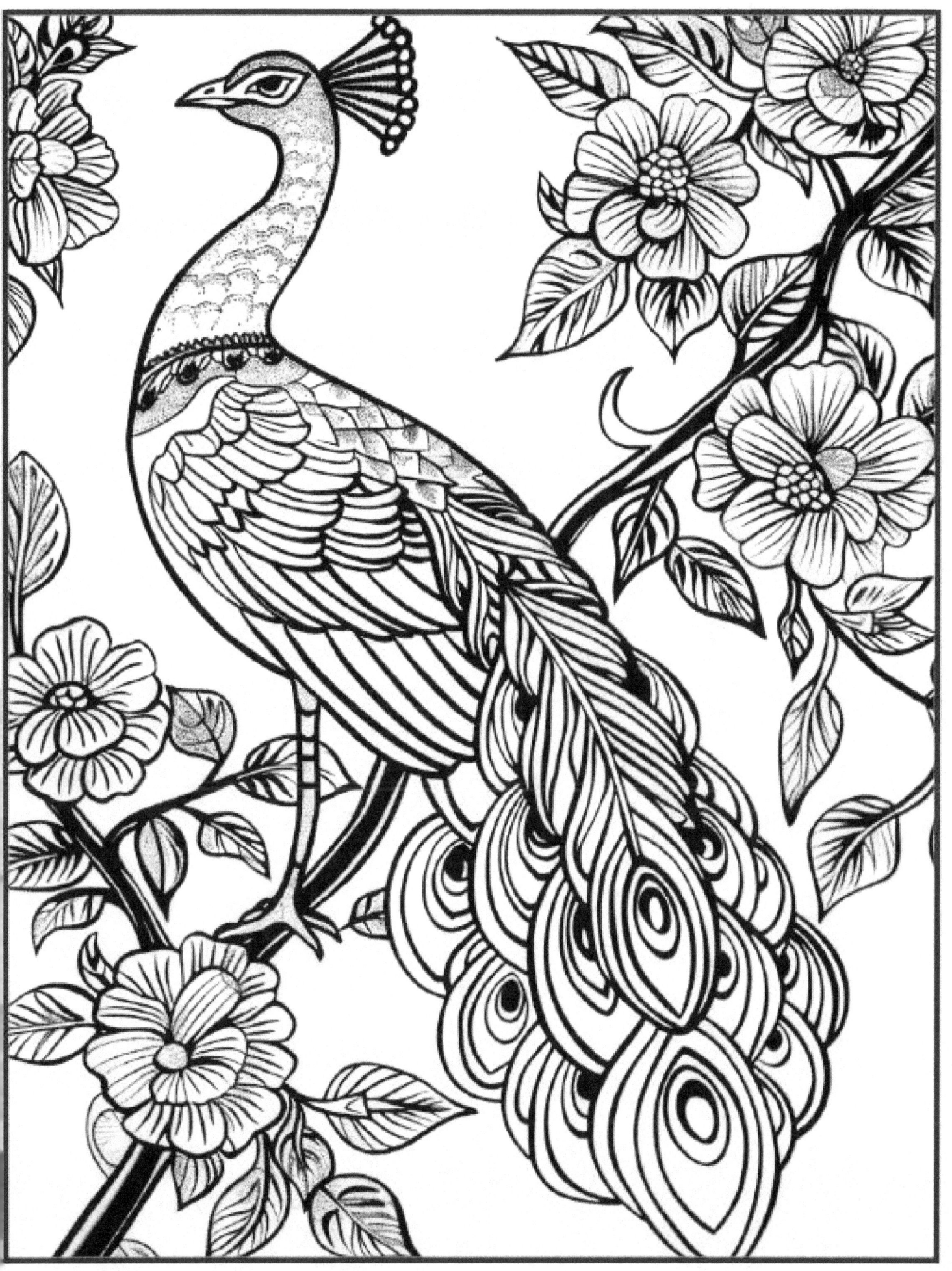

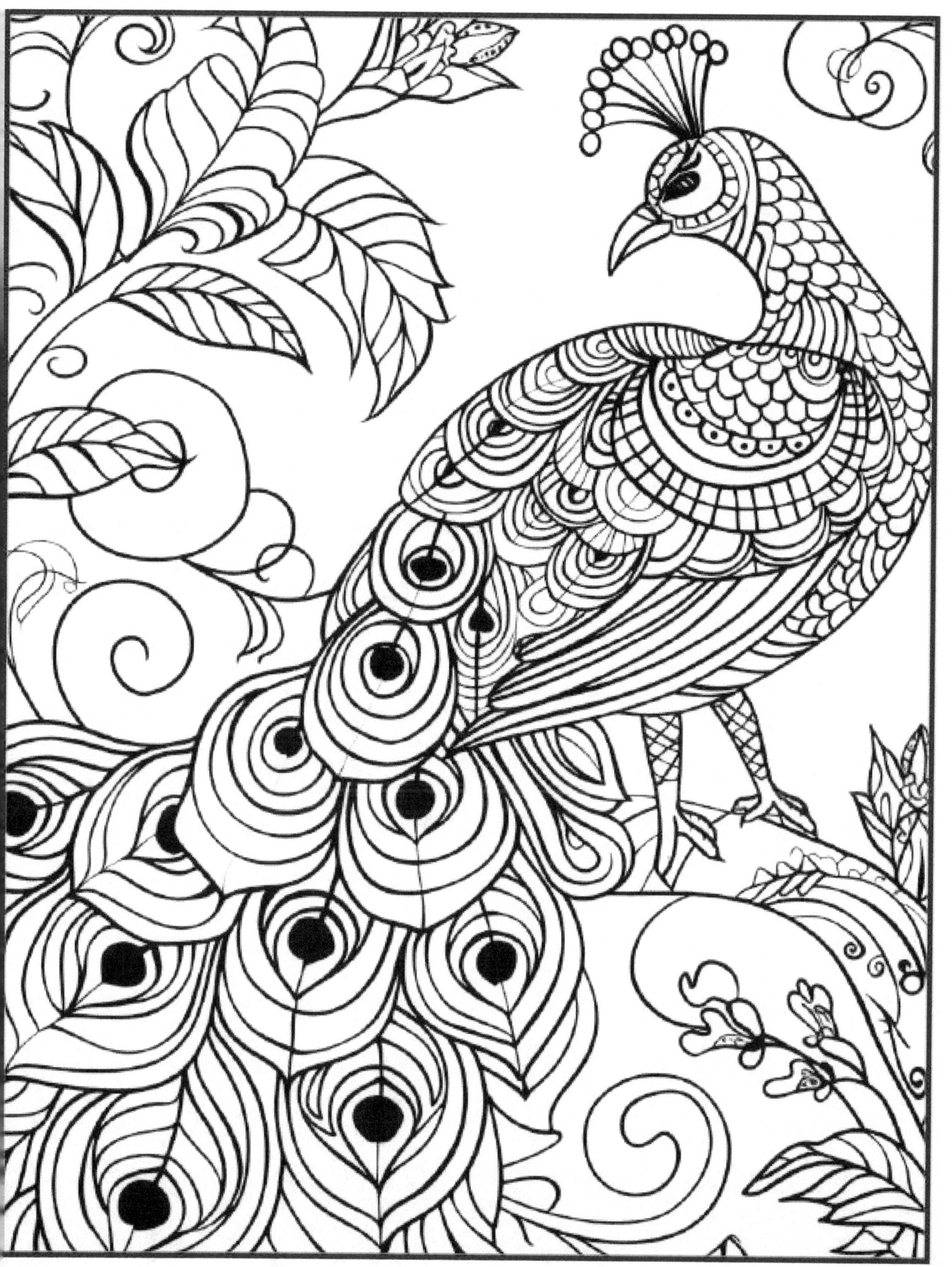

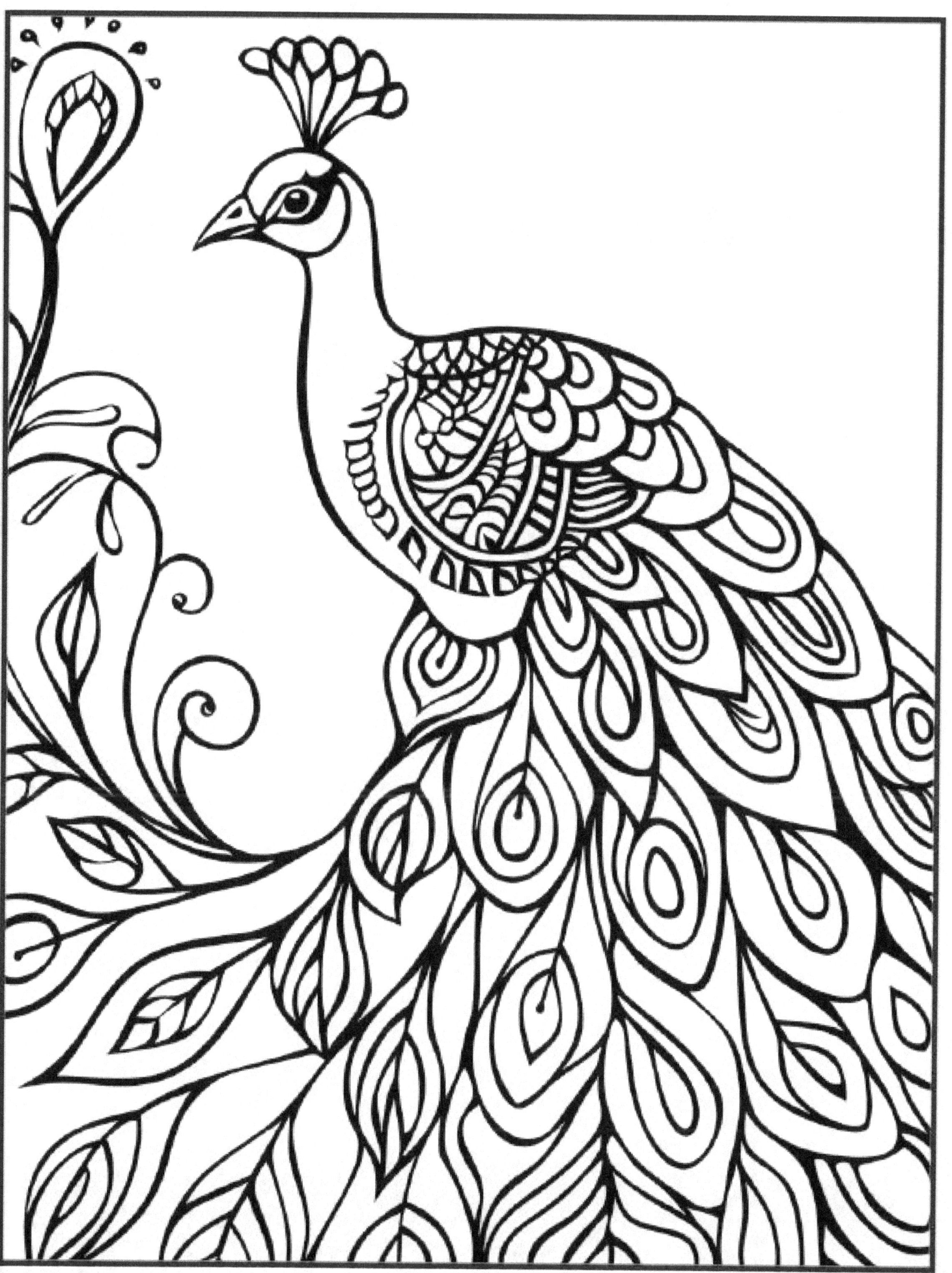

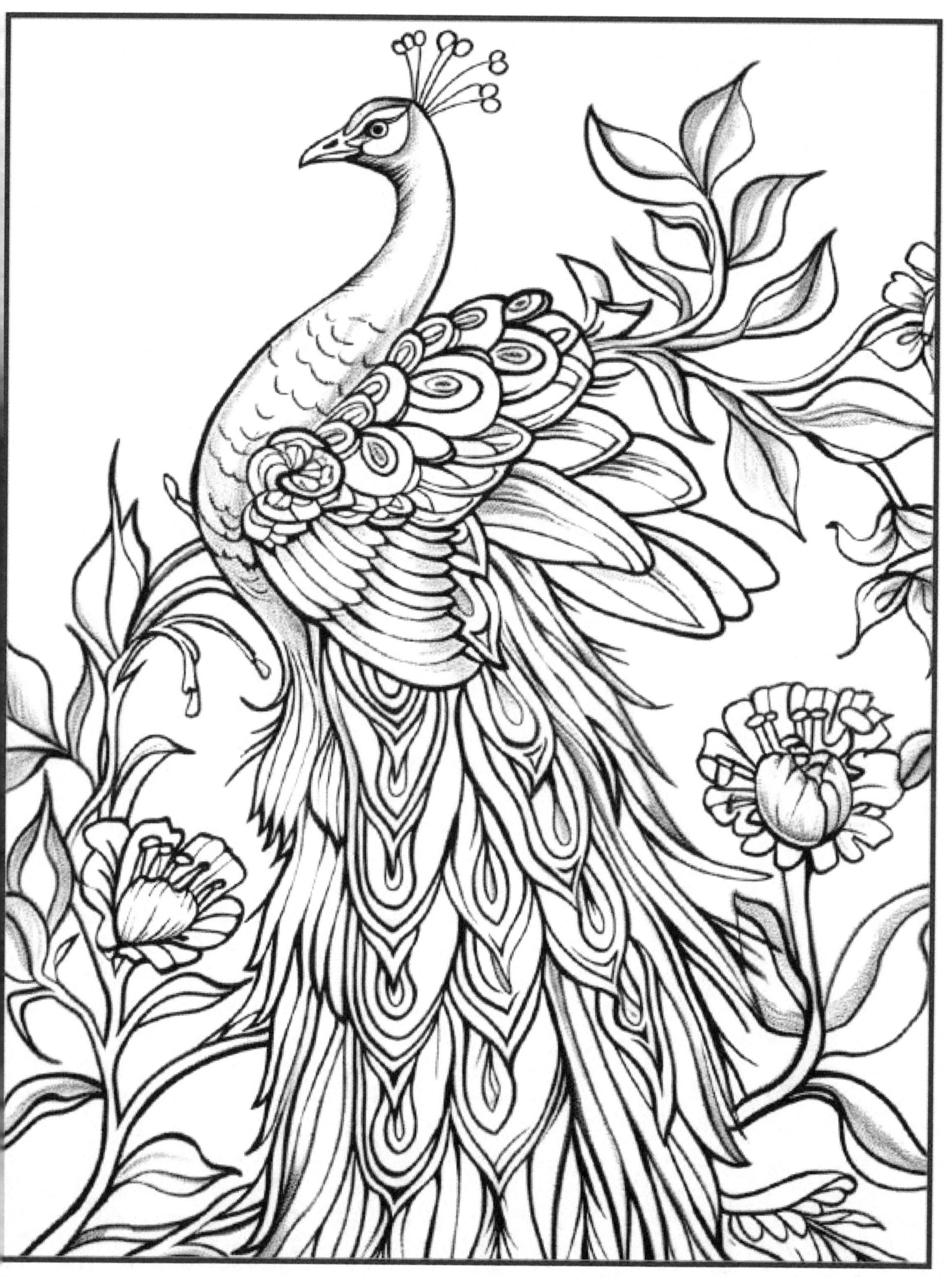

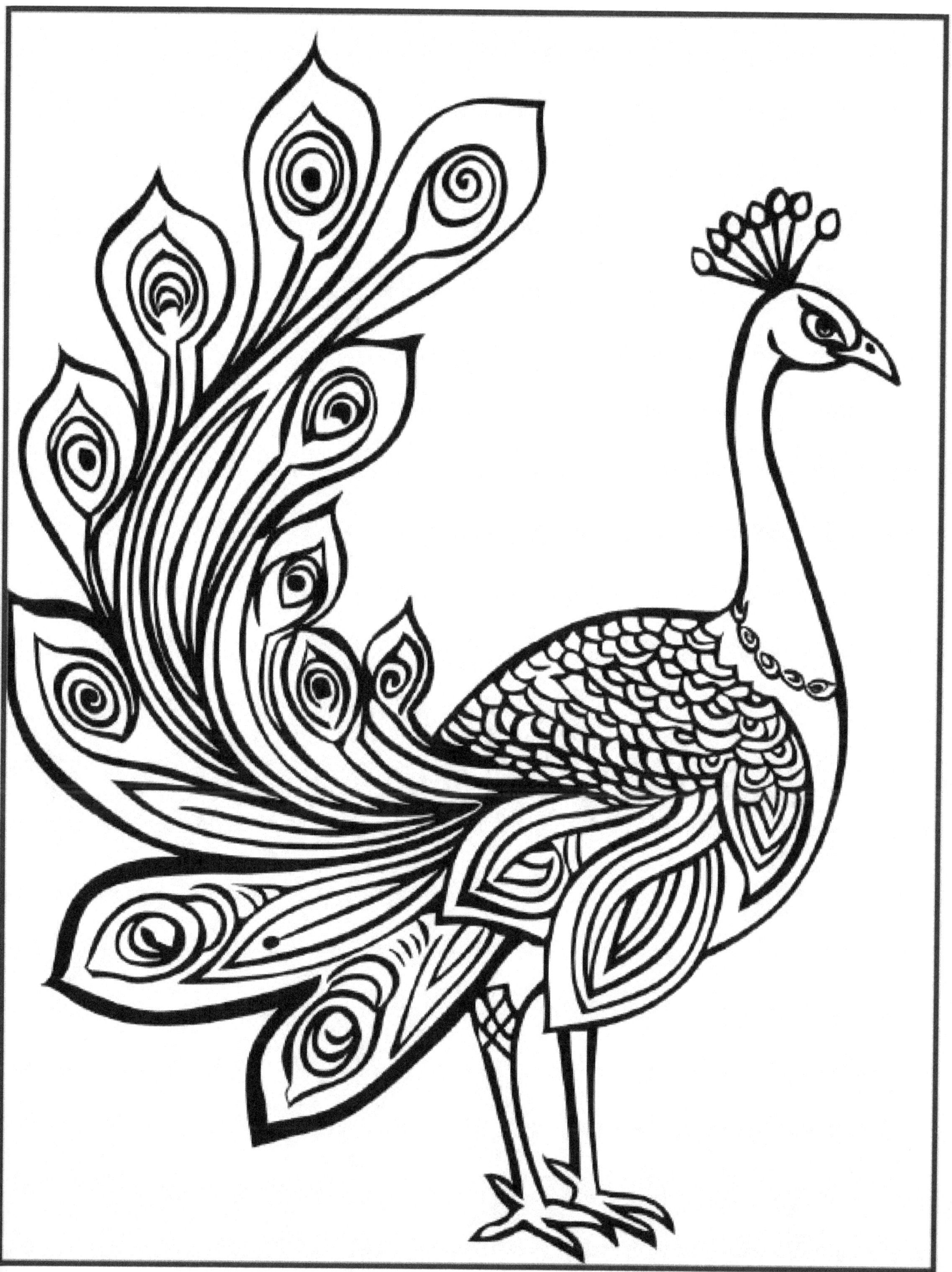

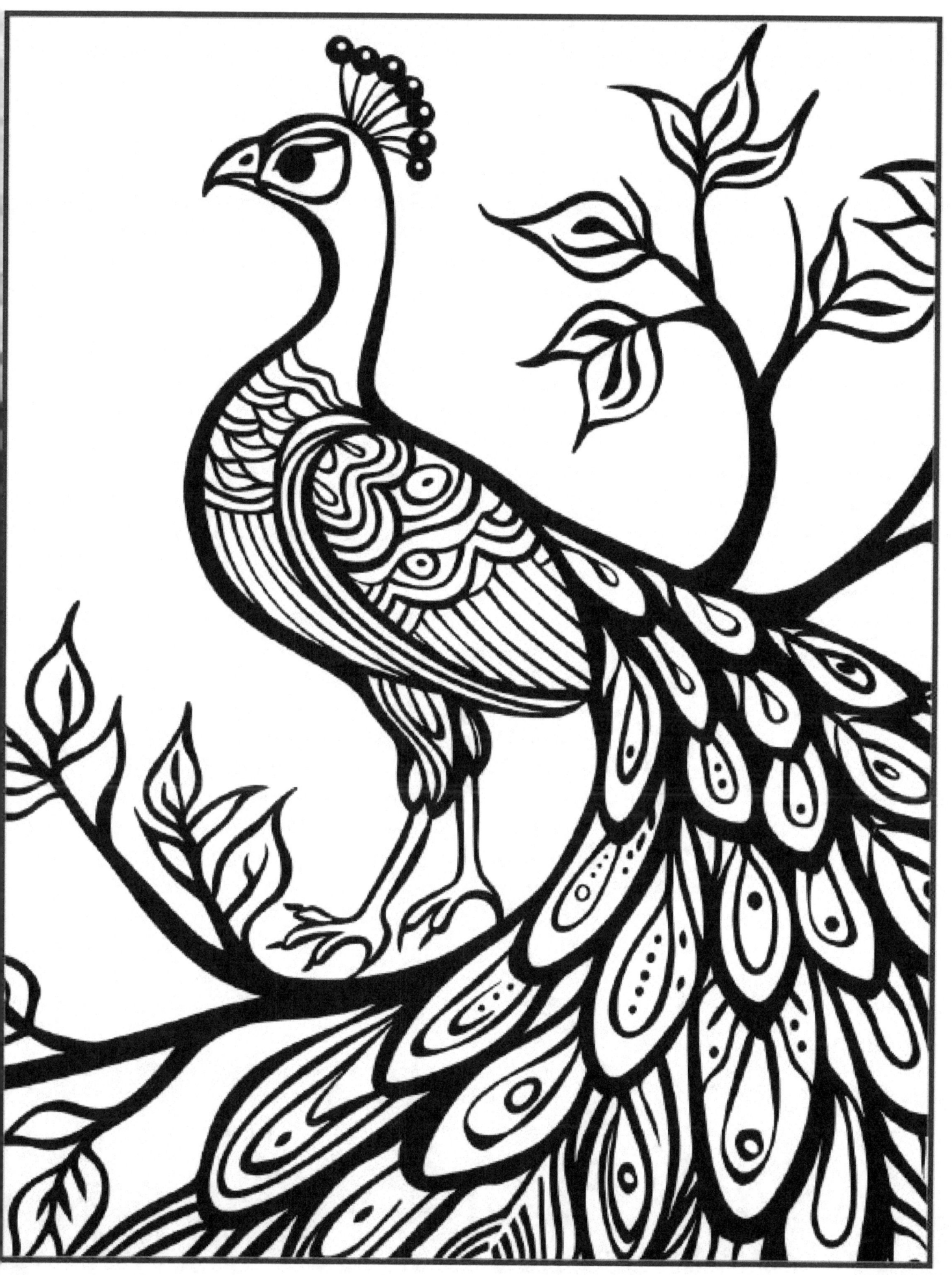

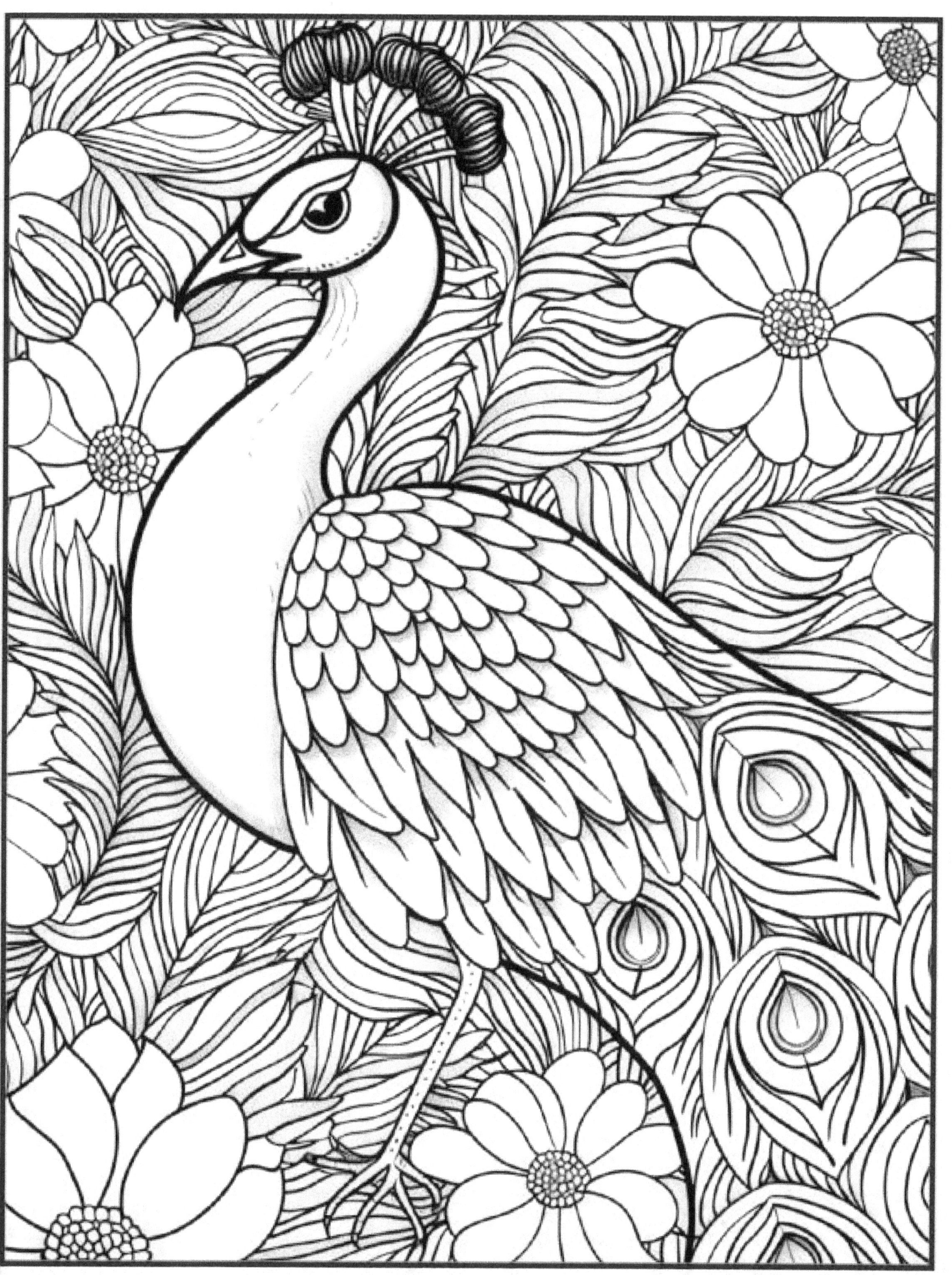

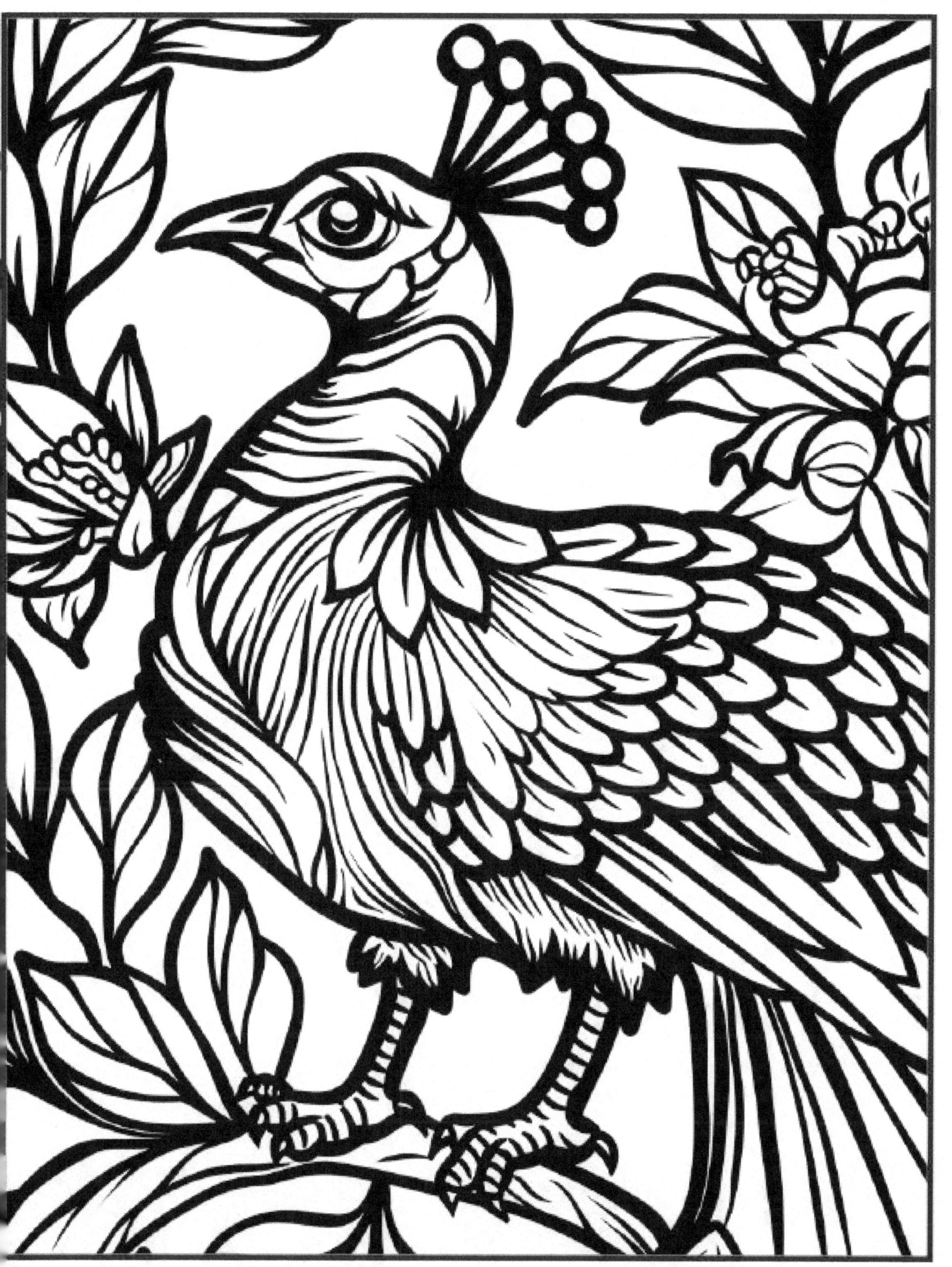

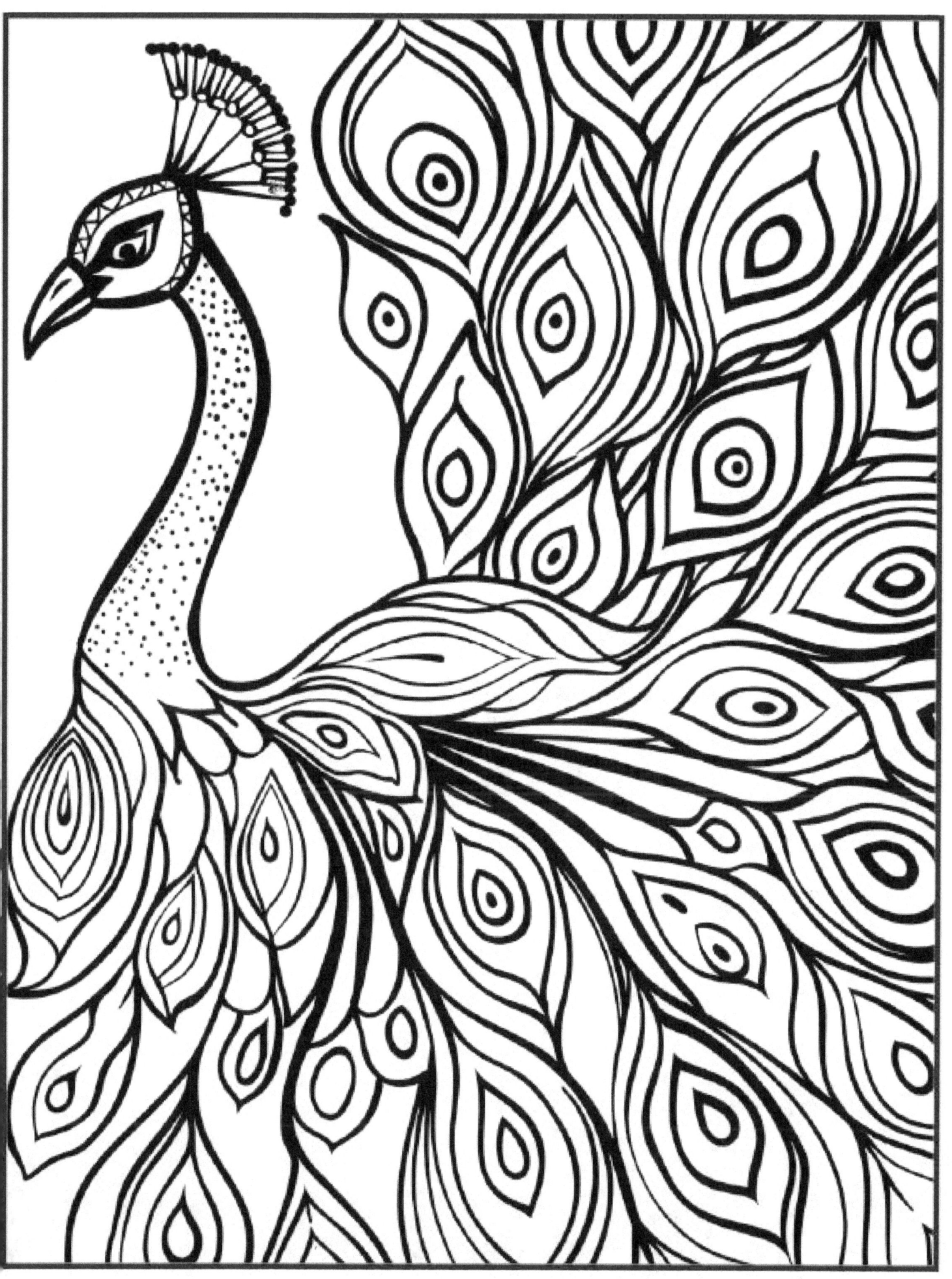

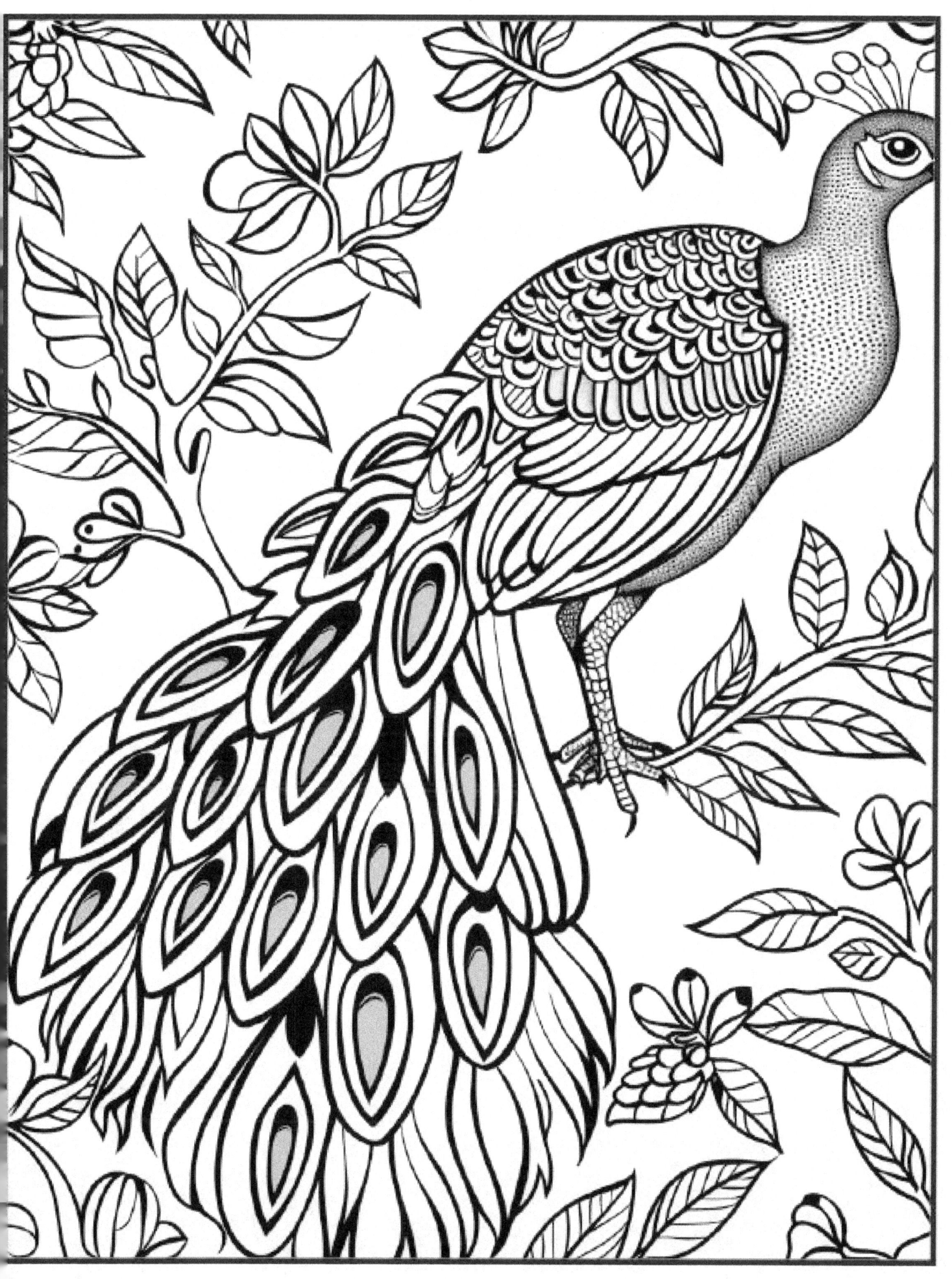

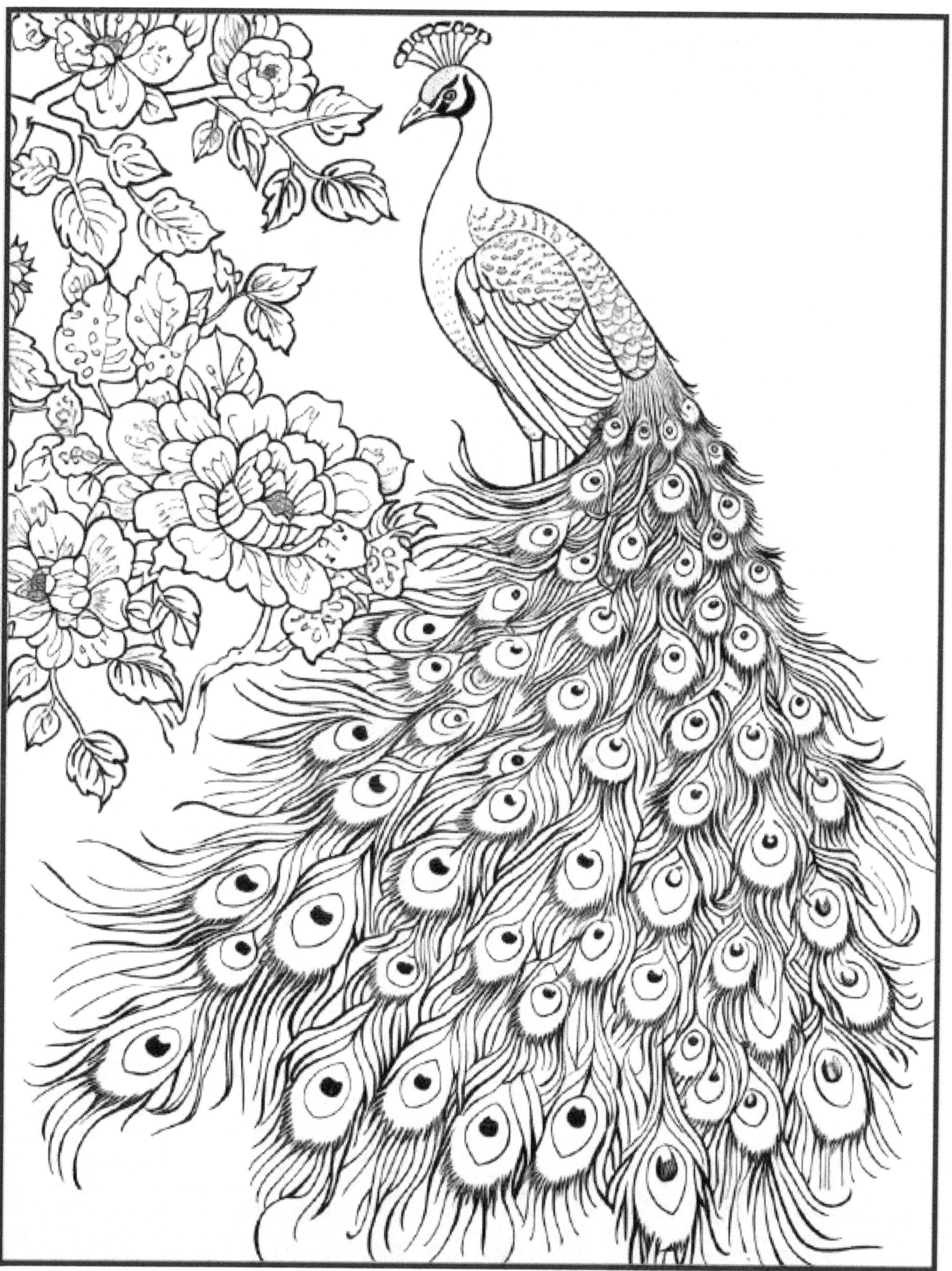

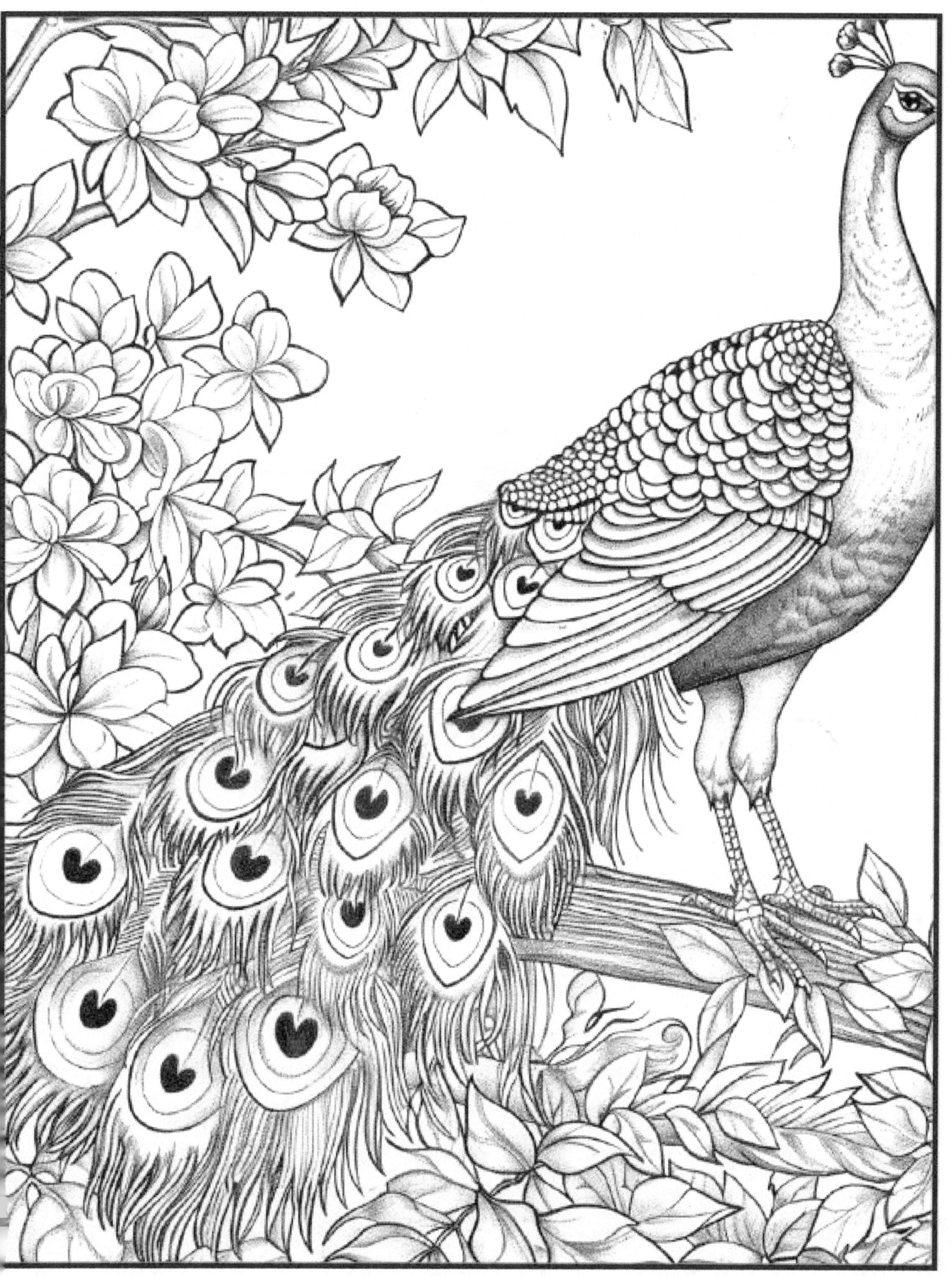

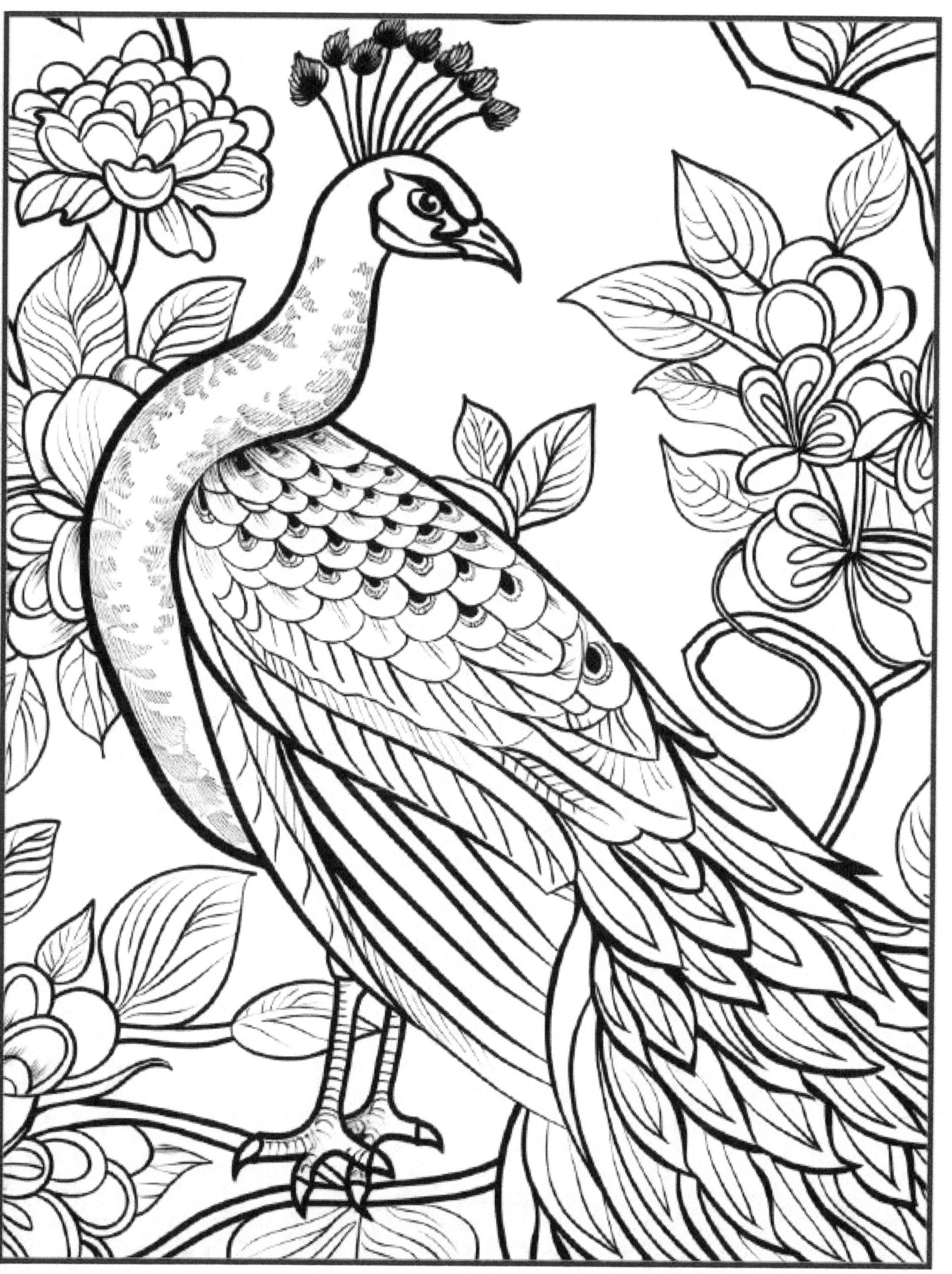

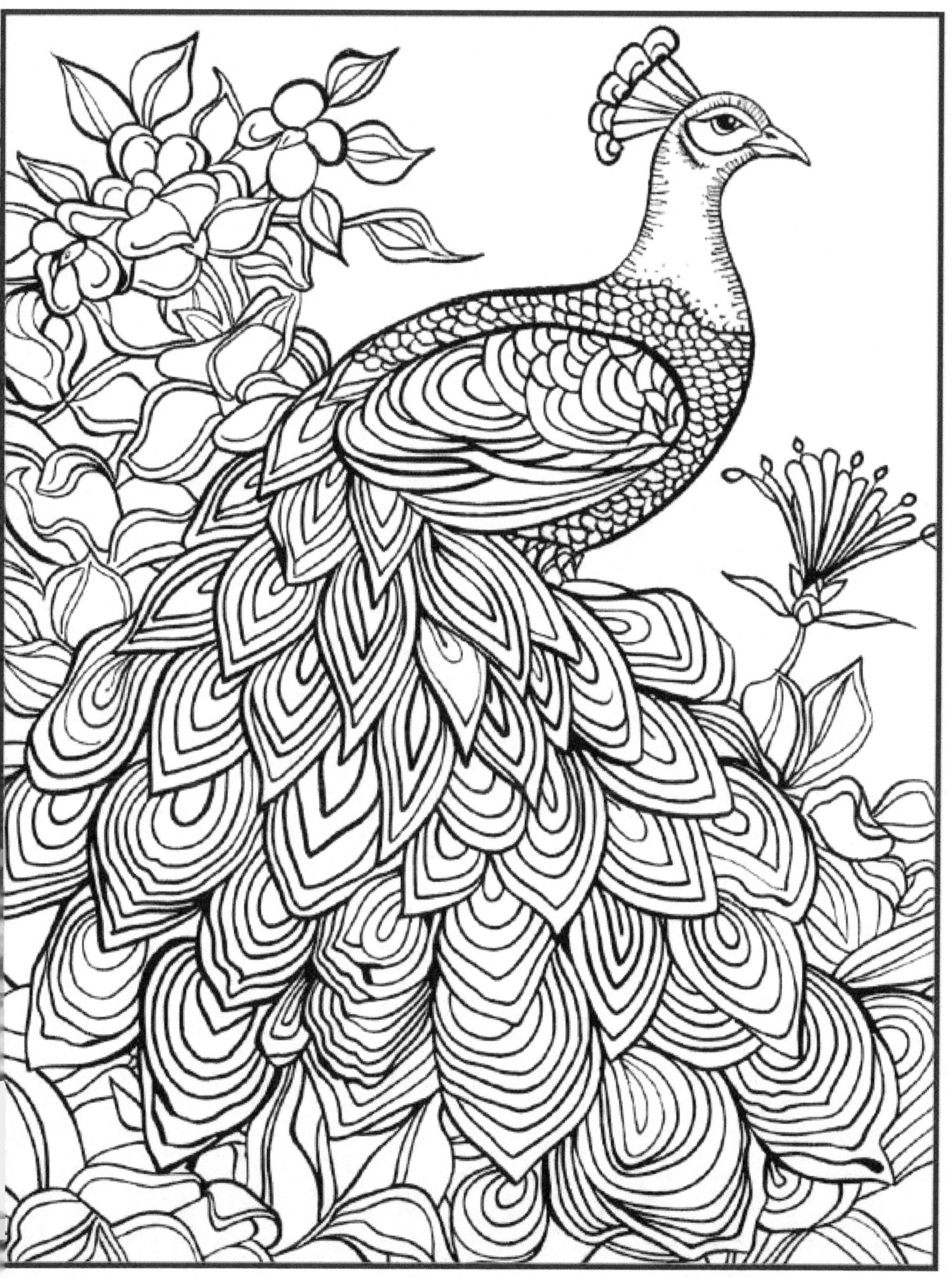

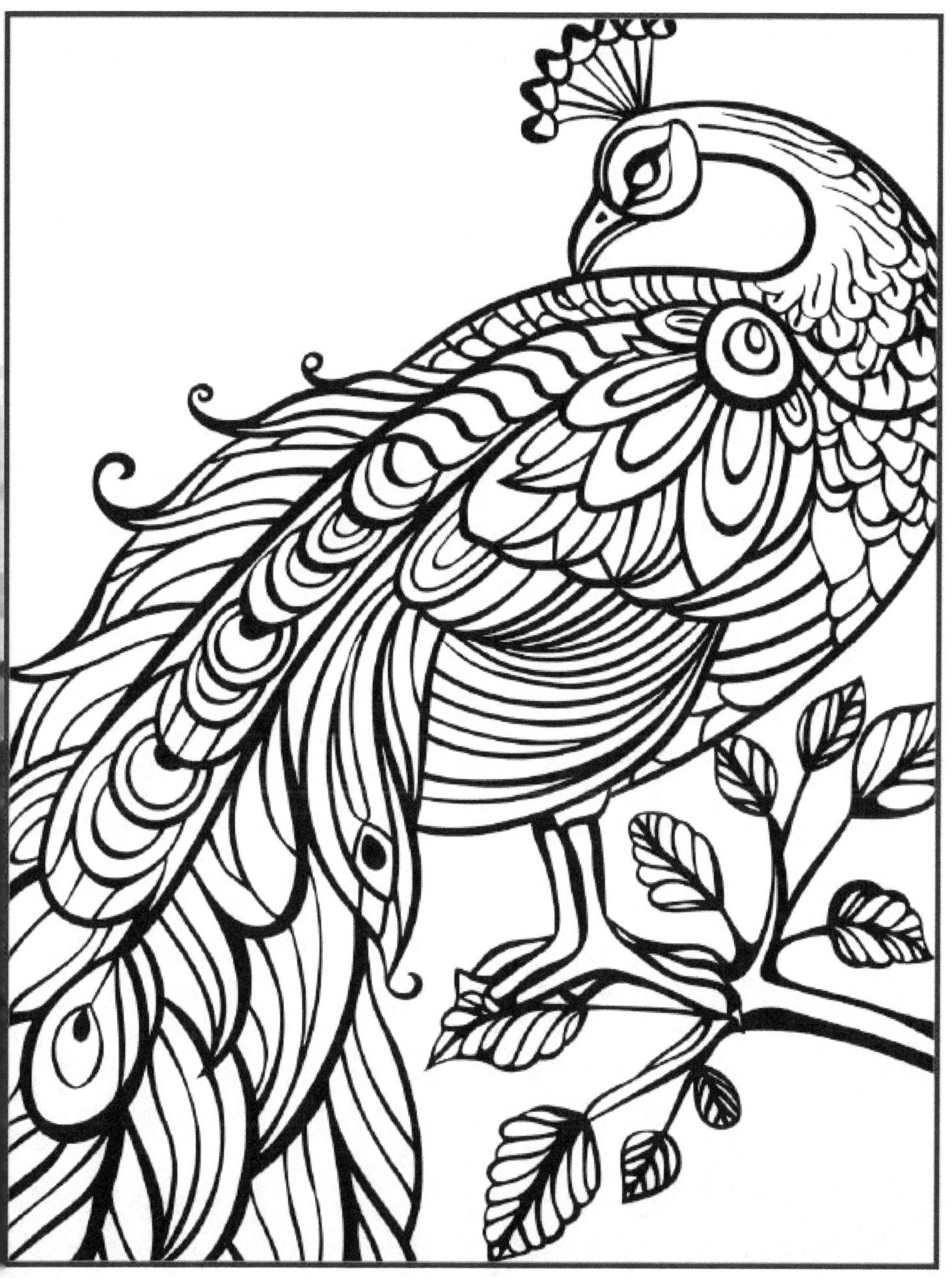

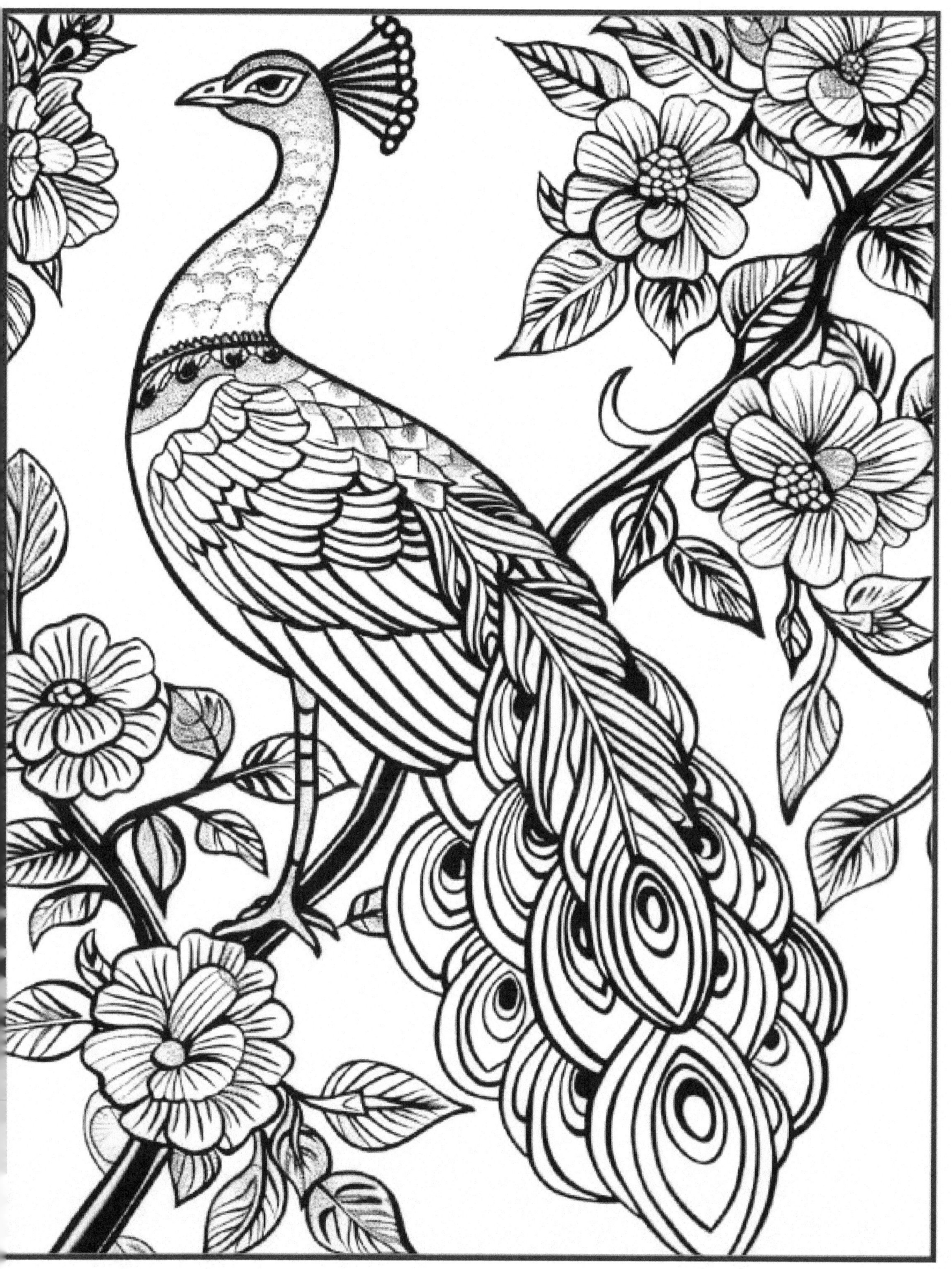

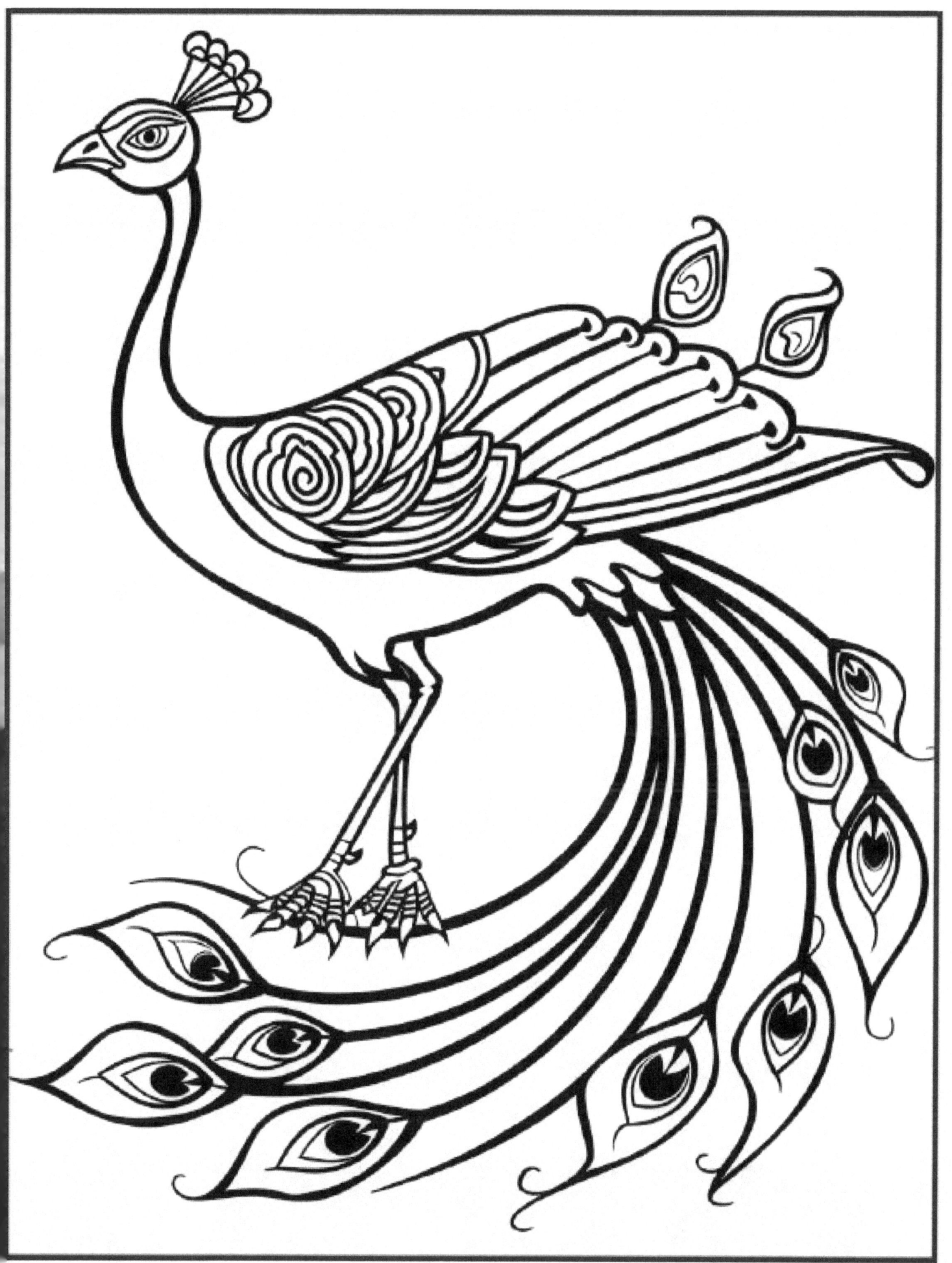

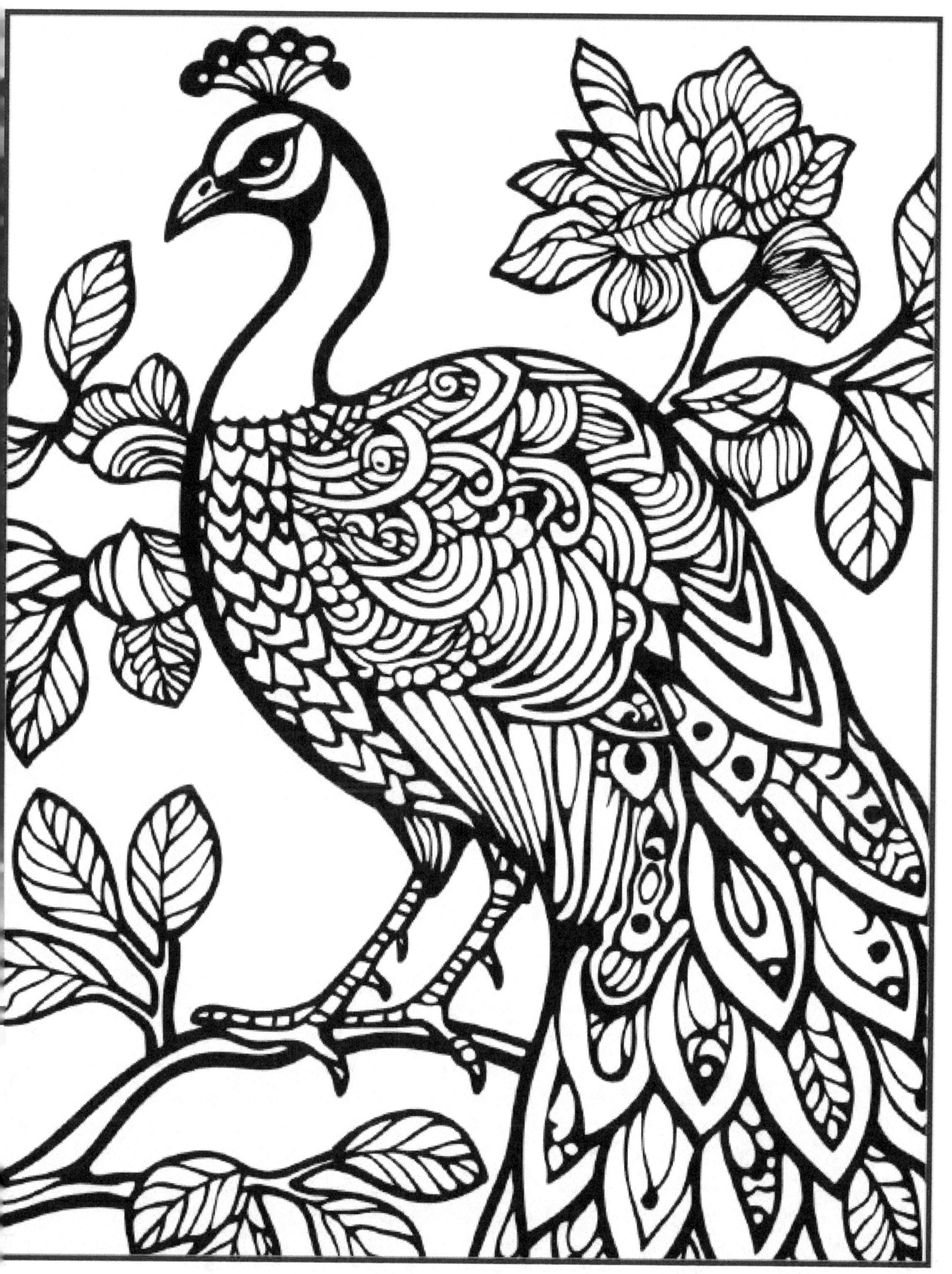

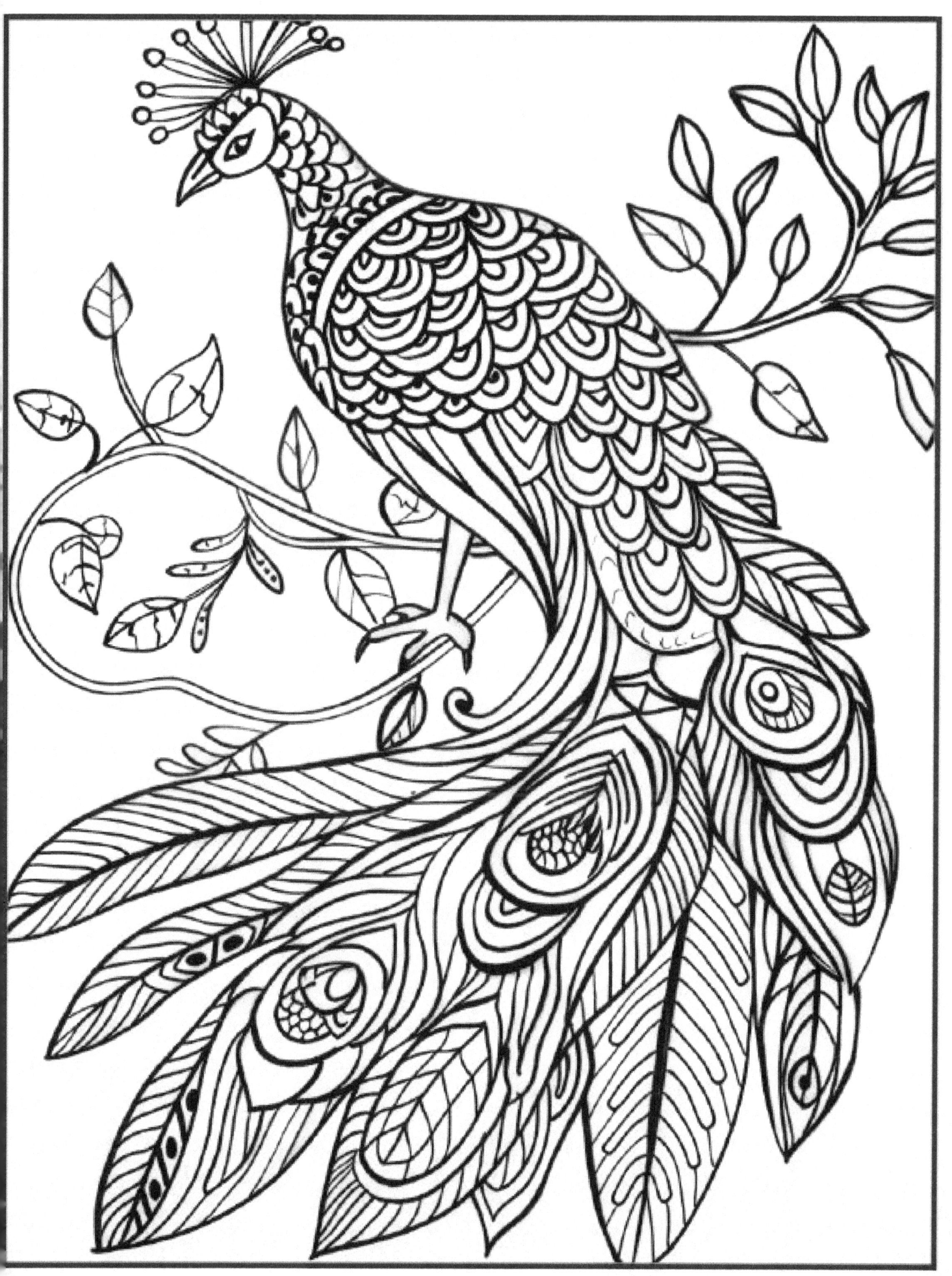

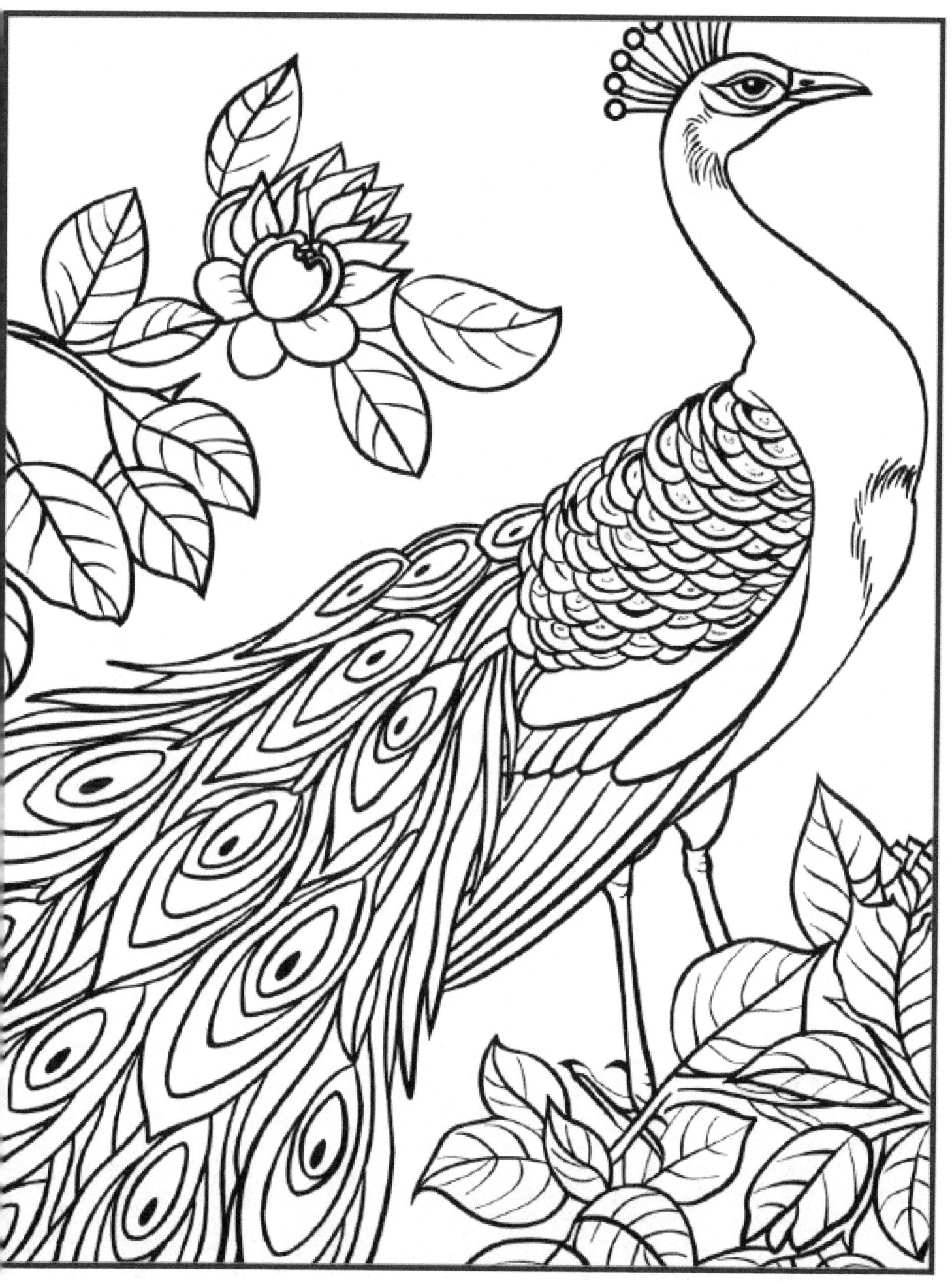

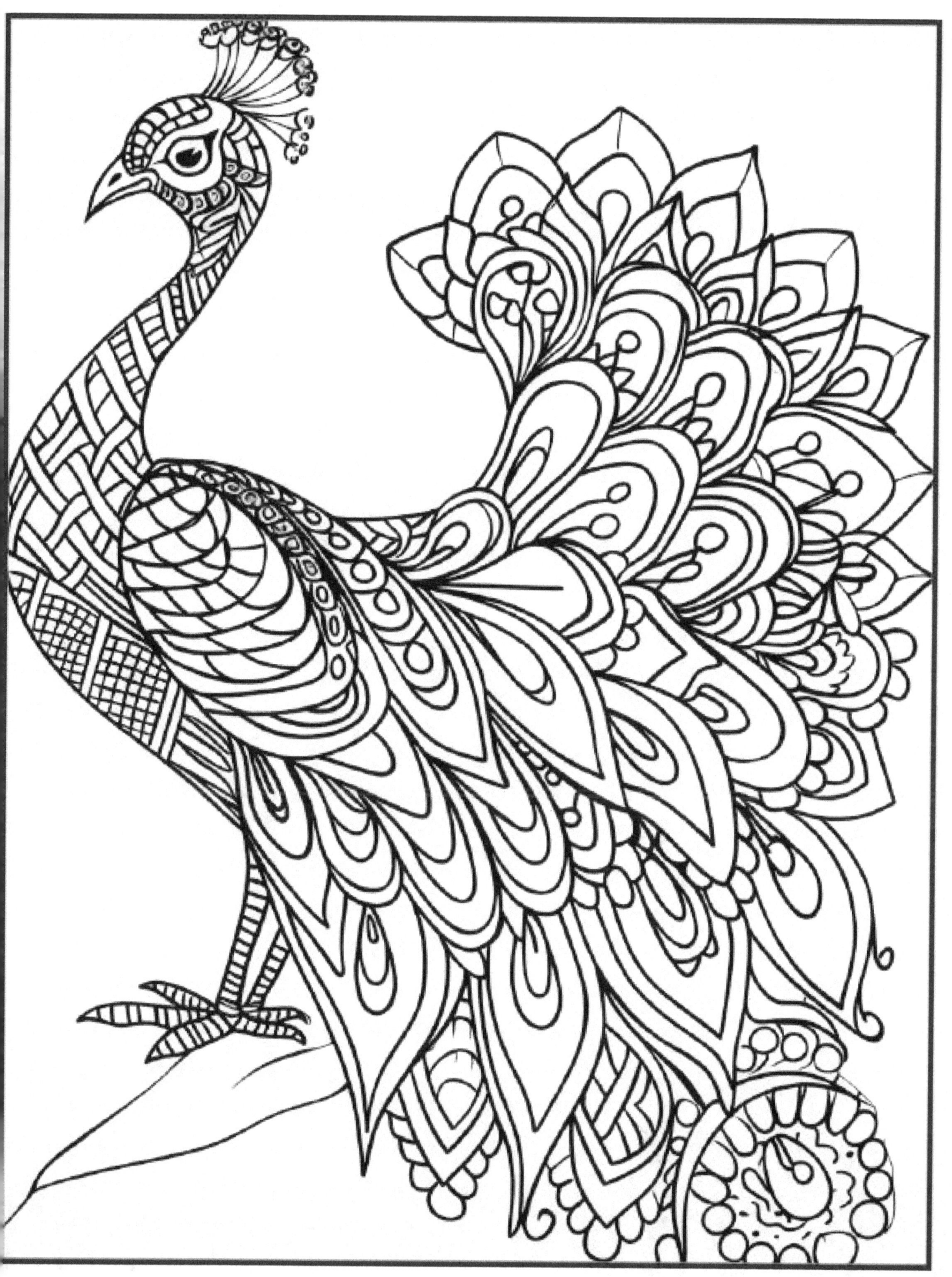

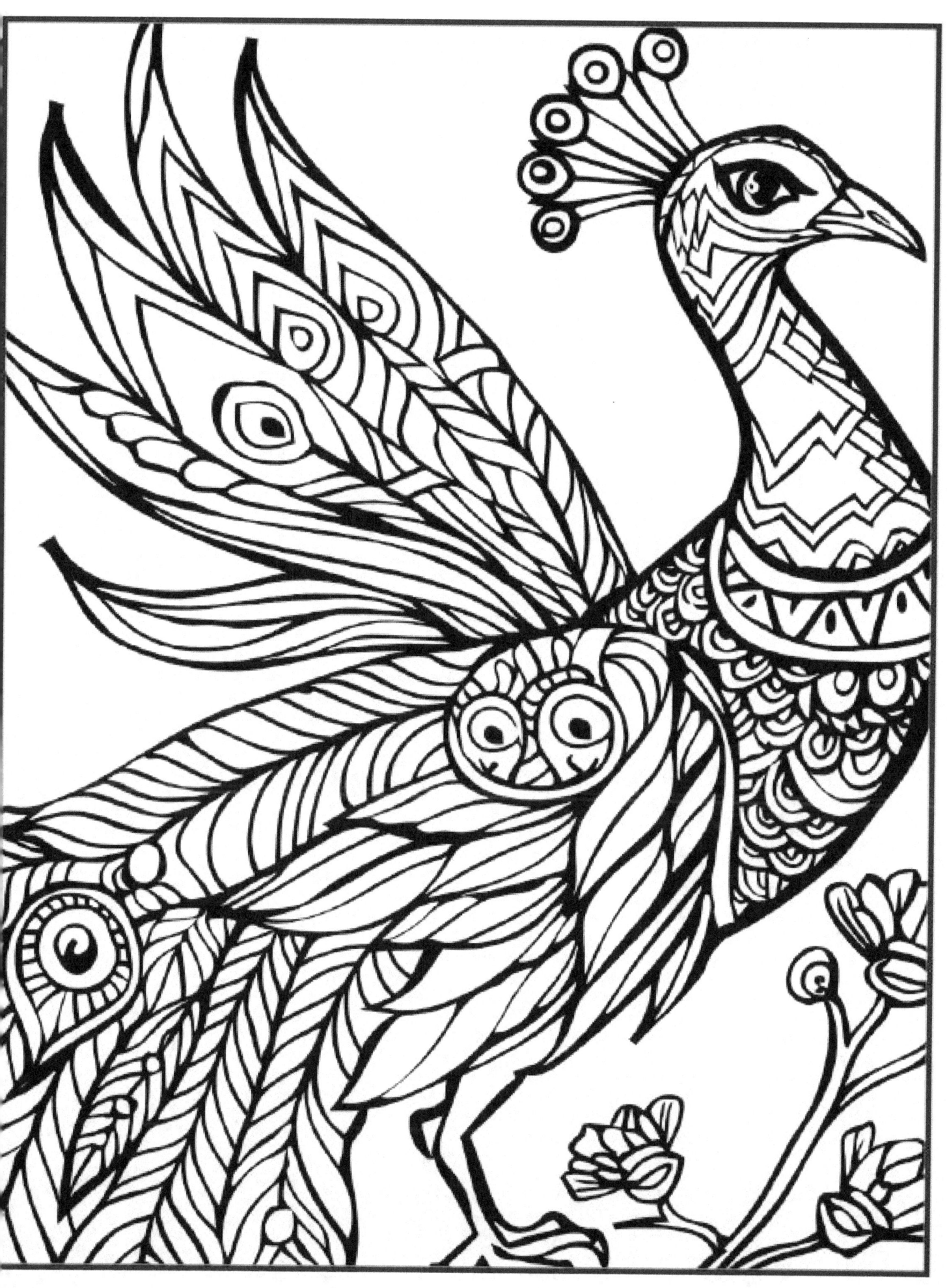

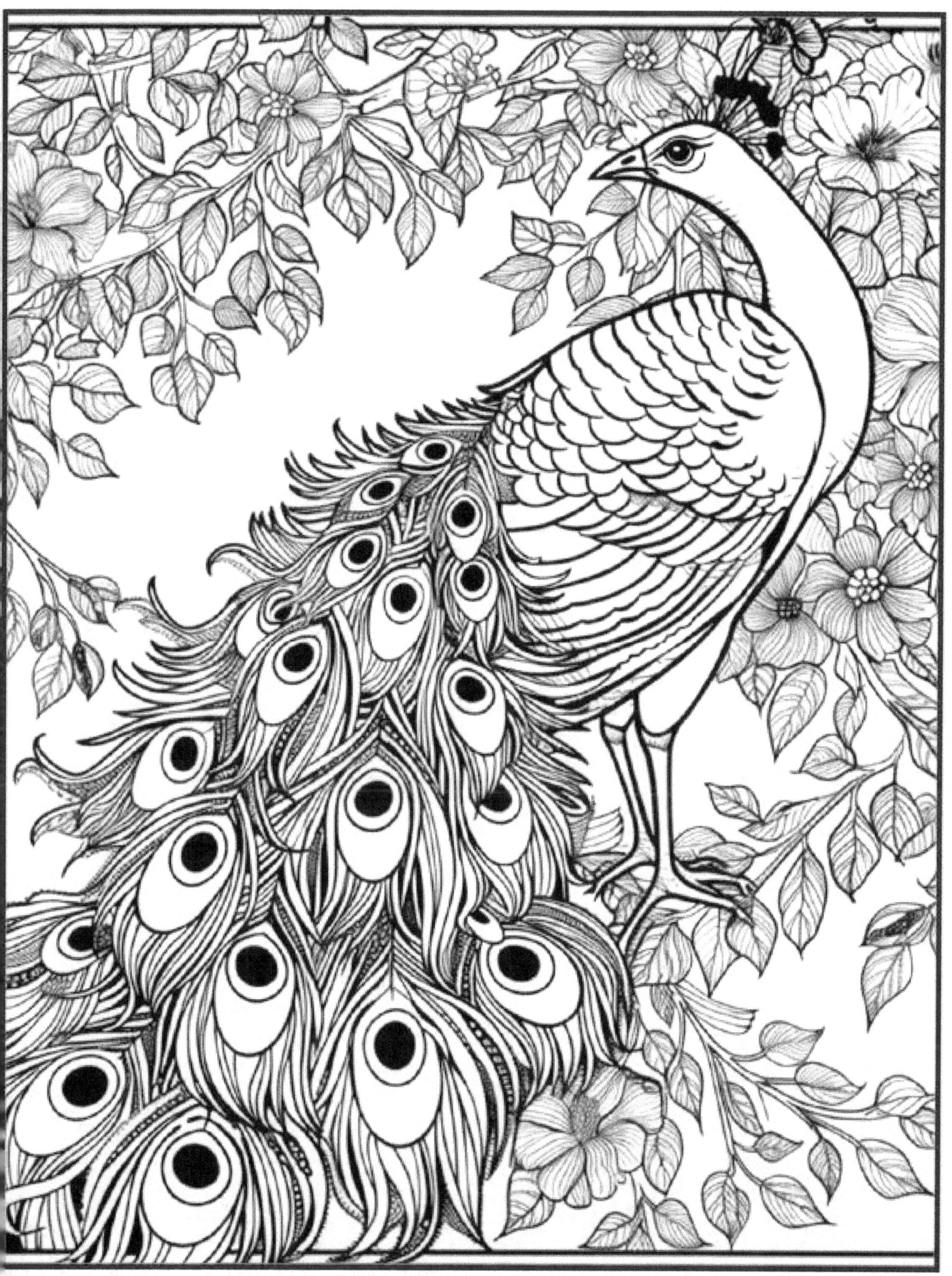

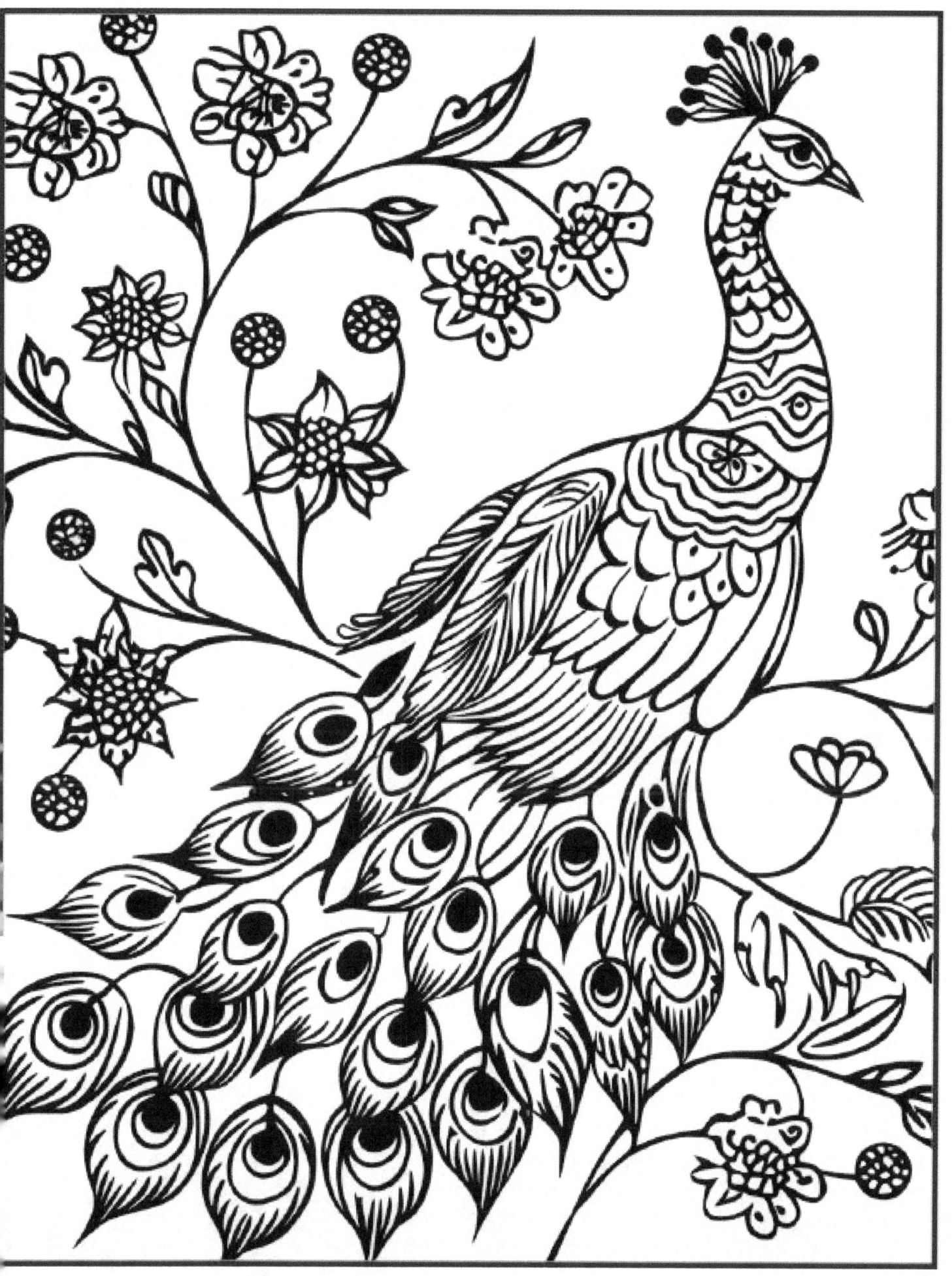

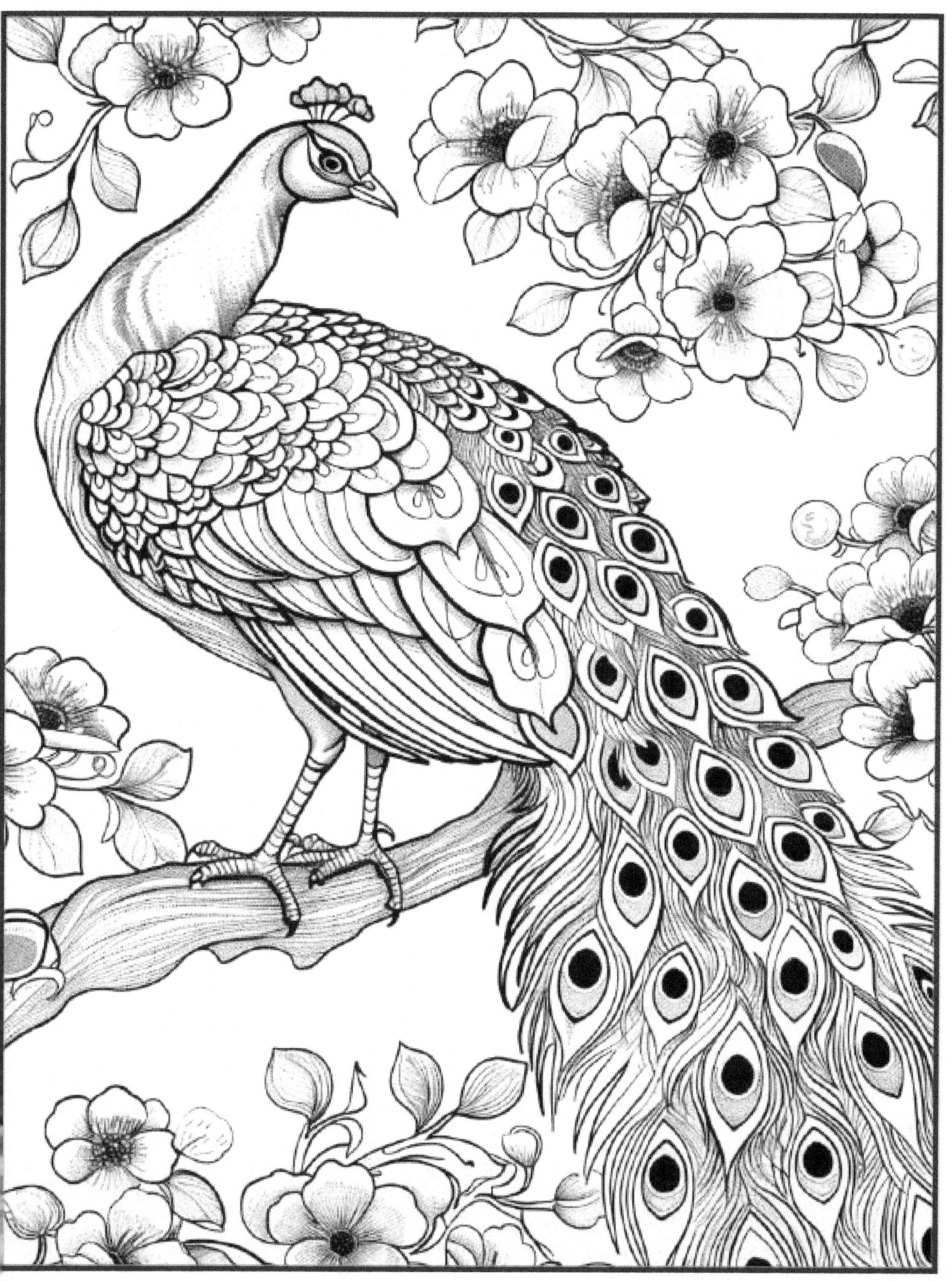

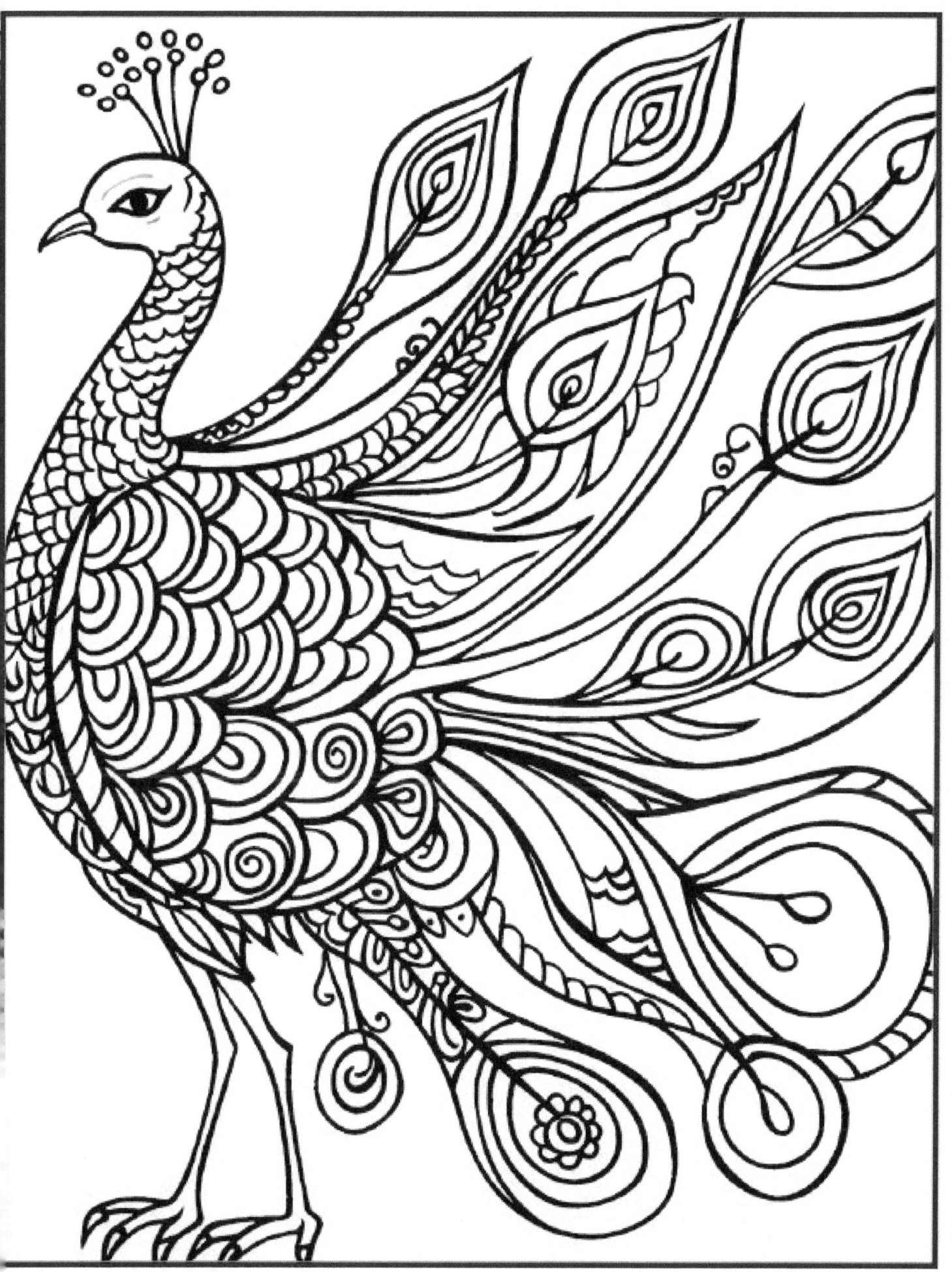

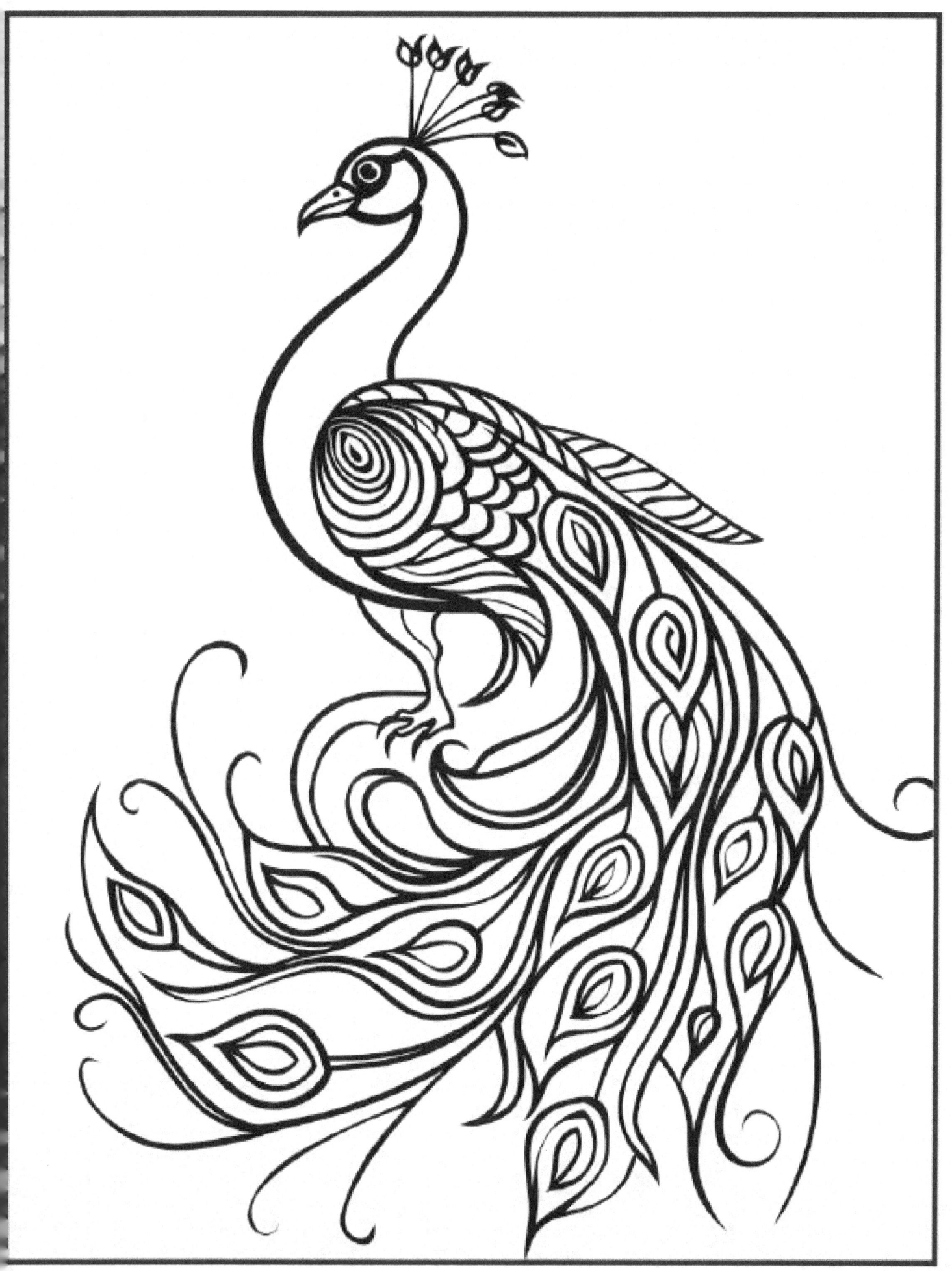

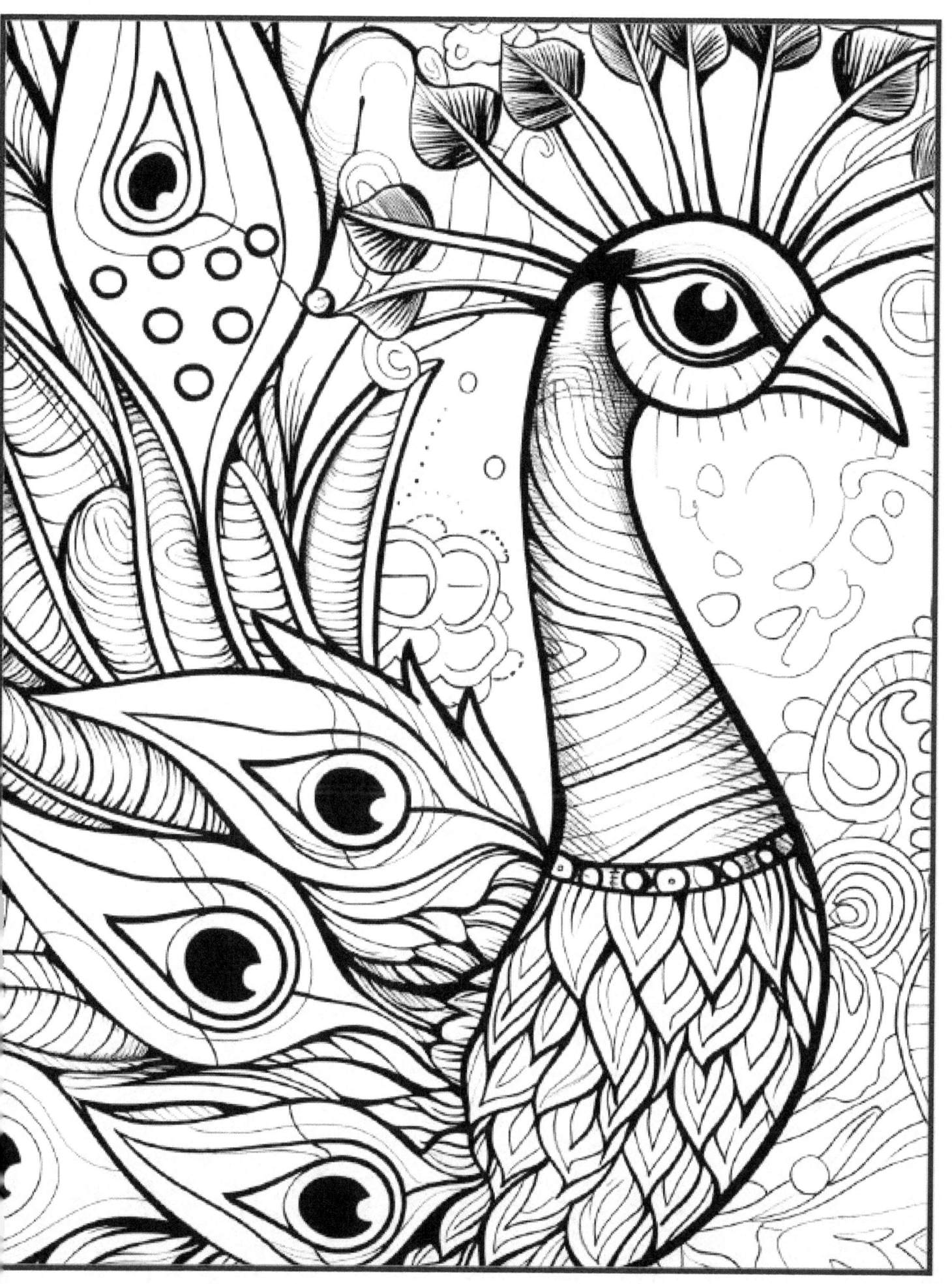

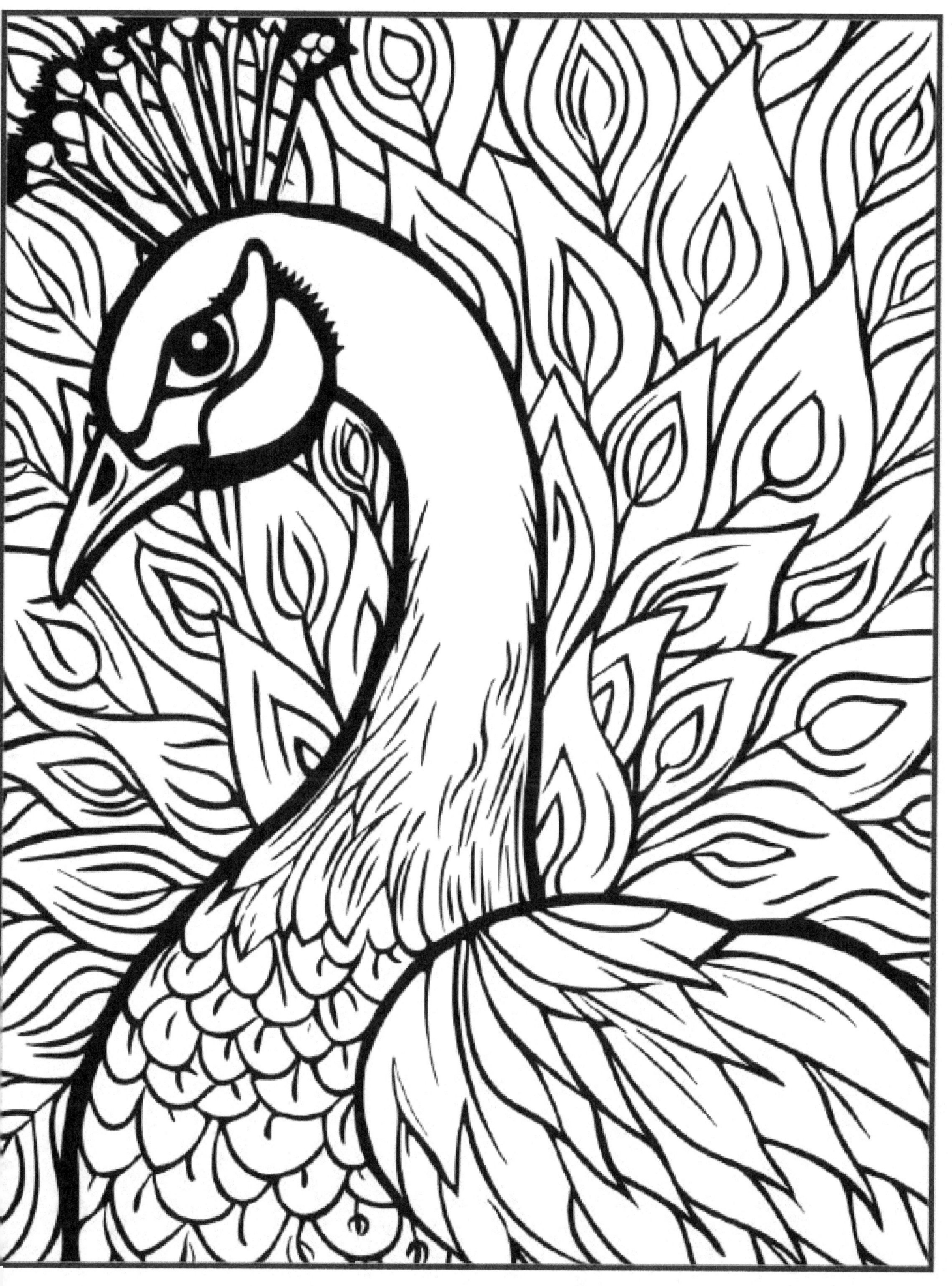

ColorQuest Collections

Fun and creative coloring books

Calming | Relaxing | Stress Relief

For more fun and creative coloring books, search for ColorQuest Collections in your favorite bookstore!

Copyright 2023. All rights reserved. No part of this book or this book as a whole may be used, reproduced, or transmitted in any form or means without written permission from the publisher.

Thank you

PLEASE LEAVE US A REVIEW!

IF YOU ENJOYED THIS COLORING BOOK, PLEASE TAKE A MOMENT TO LEAVE A REVIEW. YOUR FEEDBACK HELPS US IMPROVE AND GUIDES OTHER CREATIVE SPIRITS TO THEIR PERFECT COLORING ADVENTURE!

SCAN HERE

FOR MORE CREATIVE COLORING BOOKS, PLEASE SEARCH FOR COLORQUEST COLLECTIONS IN YOUR FAVORITE BOOKSTORE!

COLORQUEST COLLECTIONS

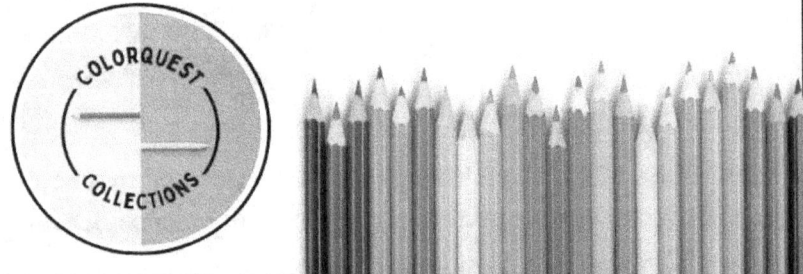